the smart approach to®

window
DECOR

Third Edition

CREATIVE
HOMEOWNER®

the smart approach to®

window
DECOR

Third Edition

Lynn Elliott and Lisa Lent

CREATIVE HOMEOWNER®, Upper Saddle River, New Jersey

THE SMART APPROACH TO® WINDOW DECOR, THIRD EDITION

SENIOR EDITOR	Kathie Robitz
PHOTO RESEARCHER	Robyn Poplasky
ADDITIONAL PHOTO EDITING	Stan Sudol
EDITORIAL ASSISTANTS	Jennifer Calvert, Nora Grace
EDITORIAL INTERN	Kealan Bakke
INDEXER	Schroeder Indexing Services
FRONT COVER PHOTOGRAPHY	Jessie Walker
INSIDE FRONT COVER PHOTOGRAPHY	*top* Mark Samu; *bottom* Mark Lohman
BACK COVER PHOTOGRAPHY	*top* Mark Samu; *center* Eric Roth; *bottom* Nancy Hill
INSIDE BACK COVER PHOTOGRAPHY	davidduncanlivingston.com

CREATIVE HOMEOWNER

VICE PRESIDENT AND PUBLISHER	Timothy O. Bakke
PRODUCTION DIRECTOR	Kimberly H. Vivas
ART DIRECTOR	David Geer
MANAGING EDITOR	Fran J. Donegan

Current Printing (last digit)
10 9 8 7 6 5 4 3 2 1

The Smart Approach to® Window Decor, Third Edition
Library of Congress Control Number: 2007922556
ISBN-10: 1-58011-365-6
ISBN-13: 978-1-58011-365-6

CREATIVE HOMEOWNER®
A Division of Federal Marketing Corp.
24 Park Way
Upper Saddle River, NJ 07458
www.creativehomeowner.com

acknowledgments

Sincere thanks to all of those who generously offered their assistance, especially the staffs at Windows of Montclair and Country Curtains as well as the American Society of Interior Designers (ASID). Recognition must also go to Anne Marie Soto for her contribution. On a personal note, a special thank you to Dolores and John Elliott for their unfailing support.

contents

introduction

Selecting the right window treatment can be confusing. There are so many things to consider: the architecture of the window, the style of the room, your lifestyle and budget, and how you want the window treatment to look and function. And like any other aspect of good design, dressing a window takes a concentrated effort to get it right. That's how *The Smart Approach to® Window Decor* can help.

By presenting a wide range of window-treatment types and styles, the book provides lots of ideas that can inspire your own design. But more than that, *The Smart Approach to® Window Decor* walks you through the decision-making process—step-by-step. It helps you to see the "big picture" by first analyzing the structure of the window and its place within the architecture, then showing you how to take that information and study it alongside the other decorative elements of your home.

Once you've mastered that, you'll be ready to tackle the questions of lifestyle and budget, which should help you decide whether or not to go the custom route. "Smart Tips" scattered throughout the book offer handy decorator advice, too.

Whichever you choose, custom window treatments or ready-made ones, you'll find the chapters that explore the various types of coverings—curtains and draperies; shades, blinds, and shutters; and cornices, valances, and swags—insightful, particularly when they are combined with the advice for choosing a fabric. If you're looking for a way to add flair to your design, you'll find that the discussion of the various types of decorative embellishments will show you how to add rich details. When you're ready to install your new window treatment, Chapter 10, "Designer Hardware," starting on page 158, will explain how to select the right type of mounting device.

Some types of windows are challenging to dress because of their size, shape, or location. Chapter 11, "Problem Solving," which begins on page 172, offers solutions to many of the most common problems that homeowners face when challenged with an awkward window placement. If you're handy with sewing projects, you'll find instructions for creating your own curtains, swags, and embellishments in Chapter 12, "Curtains You Can Make," beginning on page 190.

Finally, if you want to play with a few different looks before making up your mind, consult the Appendix on page 202. Scaled versions of various window types and numerous window-treatment styles let you try out a variety of designs so that you can see how they may look in your home. Consult the "Resource Guide," on page 216, for convenient retail information and design sources.

The Smart Approach to® Window Decor should make choosing a window treatment easy and creative—no more worrying about costly mistakes. Take it along when you're shopping or consulting a professional designer.

BELOW
In a room with Modern furnishings, sleek designs look best. Here, the floor-to-ceiling panels feature a tailored heading of neat, inverted pleats. The curtains puddle slightly at the hem.

OPPOSITE
Shimmering orange-taffeta curtains bring rich, spicy color into this room, which mixes European with Near Eastern antiques. The drapery hardware is hidden behind a strip of crown molding.

1

the big picture

FORM FOLLOWS FUNCTION
DESIGN WORKBOOK

Selecting a window treatment provides you with an opportunity to make changes that can affect a room's style, how you use the room, and your level of comfort. When you think of the important role a window treatment plays, consider a number of factors. Do you need to control sunlight and glare? Heat gain or heat loss? Do you want to obscure an undesirable view or create privacy? Can you use the window treatment to modify or enhance the architectural elements of the space? Can you use it to set a mood or bring color, pattern, or texture into a room?

Of course, the right window treatment can do all of these things—and for a relatively affordable investment. In addition, it can instantly freshen a dated look or create a major focal point in an otherwise plain room. Here's how to find the right one for your needs.

A Roman shade and floor-length draperies echo the room's rich orange accent color and highlight its architectural elements.

form follows function

Today, there is a wide selection of window treatments and materials to address any or all of these concerns. Because conditions of light, heat, and lifestyle dictate changes over the course of the day or even from season to season, it's wise to select a style that is easily adjustable. For example, natural light that streams over your shoulder, while you sit in a chair with your back to the window, is lovely for reading a book. However, if you're working at a computer that is in the direct path of harsh sunlight, the glare on the monitor caused by the sun's reflection will make it difficult to read what's on the screen and may strain your eyes. A window covering that can be lowered or closed at will allows you to enjoy natural light when you want it or close it out when you don't.

Before getting started on your window-decor project, go over the following steps to make sure that you're contemplating a window treatment that does the job you need it to do.

smart steps
proceed thoughtfully

Step 1 CONSIDER VENTILATION AND AIRFLOW

Sometimes you'll want to open your windows to let in fresh air and release indoor pollutants. On occasion, you may prefer a natural breeze to an air conditioner. So choose a covering that won't impede the flow of air into the room. On the other hand, if the windows are a source for draughts or heat collection, consider purchasing insulated curtains that can cut down on these problems and may even save you the cost of replacing old windows.

RIGHT
When the view is too nice to cover up but privacy and sun control are important factors, opt for window shades. The sleek woven-wood shades featured here look great whether they are in a raised or lowered position.

Step 2 EXAMINE THE SIGHT LINES

What is the first thing you see when you enter a room? In most cases, it is the windows. Can you see them from outside the entry? You know what they say about first impressions, so use the window treatments to make an immediate style statement.

Step 3 LOOK OUT, LOOK IN

Do you want to take in the view? Then, you may want minimal window dressing. But what about privacy? You may feel as if you're living in a fishbowl, especially at night when the interior of the house is lit, unless your property is secluded. A treatment that's adjustable, such as curtains, shades, or blinds that open and close easily, is the solution. But don't ignore the way your window treatment looks from the outside. Choose a style that suits the overall style of your home.

Step 4 OBSERVE THE ARCHITECTURE

The window treatment you choose is the bridge from window to wall. What you select should blend harmoniously with the architecture and the home's interior design.

If there is a flaw in the design of the space, you can sometimes compensate for it with window decor. A treatment can add character that may be lacking or camouflage problems with scale and proportion.

Step 5 LOOK AT THE ROOM'S DECOR

Does it appear tired, dated, or simply unfinished? Consider how new window treatments can put a fresh face on the room.

BELOW
Hanging bright patterned drapery can add a much-needed splash of color to a room with plain white walls.

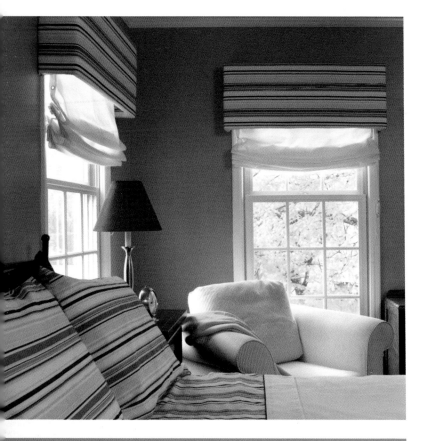

The Practical Role of a Window Treatment

When you imagine heavy, multi-layered fabric covering a window, it's usually in a period- or historic-design context. (Although lighter-weight versions are popular in traditional homes, today.) Textiles, such as lined wool, damask, silk, brocade, velvet, and tapestries, provided much-needed insulation against extreme temperatures in an era without the luxuries of double-glazed glass, central heating, and air conditioning. Though insulation is often a factor in choosing a window treatment, ventilation and controlling natural light are more common concerns, nowadays.

Any room with an eastern orientation is subject to strong morning light, a consideration acutely important in a bedroom, for example. A room with windows facing west gets strong light in the afternoon; however, if you don't ordinarily use the room at this time of day, you may not care.

North-facing rooms, because they receive no direct sunlight, get chilly, especially during the winter. This makes a good case for insulated window treatments. Spaces with a southern exposure receive the most natural light; during the summer months or in a

ABOVE LEFT
Colorful striped valances are paired with soft, light-filtering Roman shades that protect the room from strong morning sunlight.

LEFT
A layered dressing of plain panels trimmed in plaid and a soft fabric window shade provide a decorative solution to light control.

OPPOSITE
The linear quality of wood blinds complement this tailored bathroom. Blinds are also a practical choice for the bath because the slats can be raised or lowered to control privacy and ventilation.

smart tip

OPERATING THE WINDOW

Consider the way a window opens and closes before choosing a window treatment. Double-hung windows pose the fewest problems. Casement windows and French doors that swing into a room require a design that will not obstruct their paths of operation.

warm climate, these rooms can get too hot. The right window covering can abate some of the heat buildup. Think about when and where you're most likely to be affected by natural light and whether you need a means to control it.

The rays of the sun also affect furnishings, so when choosing your window treatment, keep this in mind, as well. Delicate fabrics, wallcoverings, and even wood finishes can be harmed by continuous direct exposure to strong natural light. Translucent fabric panels, once called "glass curtains," are often combined with draperies to filter sunlight.

■ **Curtains and Drapery.** Loosely hung fabric or drapery panels that are attached to the window frame or sash offer some control over both light and privacy. The level depends on how many layers are installed and whether or not the fabric is lined. Sheer fabrics allow the transmission of light and don't obscure the view to the outdoors. Sometimes curtains and drapery are not adjustable; they have to be installed with a rod system or rings that allow you to open or close the panels to efficiently control light and privacy.

■ **Shades, Blinds, and Shutters.** All three of these treatments are usually fully adjustable and offer complete light and privacy control. Each comes in a multitude of styles, and they can be installed alone or paired with curtains or drapery.

A window treatment can pull together an entire room, often unifying a design of disparate parts. It can change the style or ambiance from casual to formal or from sterile to romantic. New curtains can punch up, tone down, or blend into a color scheme, adding pattern and texture.

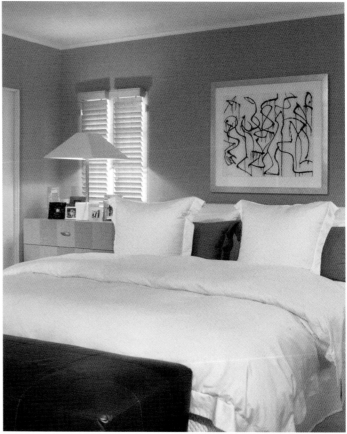

LEFT
In this child's bedroom, the wide louvers of the plantation shutters are softened by a drapery treatment that extends beyond the frame.

ABOVE
Because of their narrow size and delicate scale, miniblinds provide a great solution for this small corner bedroom window.

OPPOSITE
This sunroom's French doors feature Roman shades that can be lowered to keep the room warm in winter and cool in summer.

design workbook
PERFECT HARMONY

mix and match

A variety of textures and patterns combined with a warm color scheme give this large space a distinctive look and a cozy ambiance.

create an illusion

Dark and handsome wooden poles are placed 12 in. above the window trim to emphasize the height of the room. (See also top left.)

soften the look

Besides filtering daylight, woven matchstick blinds, along with myriad soft furnishings, add a casual feeling to this traditional-style living room.

bring in light

The combination of downlights, a vintage table lamp, and woven blinds, left, allow natural and artificial light to fill the room and reverberate in the vivid color scheme.

design workbook
CHIC AND EASY

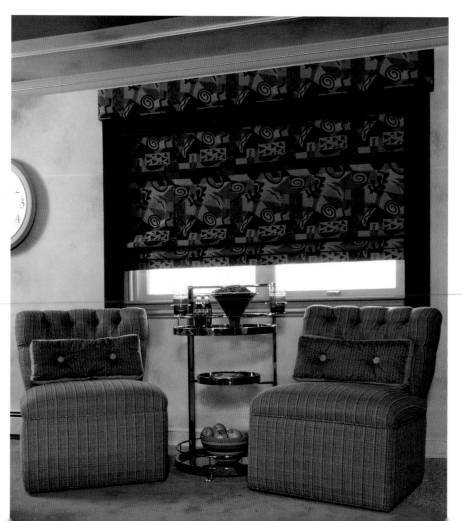

create a style

Use streamlined shades for modern decor, matchstick blinds for informal rooms, left, and Roman shades for a tailored look, bottom left.

frame it

The sleek shades in this streamlined, contemporary-style loft are mounted inside the frames to show off the crisp outline of the window.

screening the view

If your view is less than desirable, window shades can be an excellent way to regulate how much you want to see (and want seen).

furniture placement

For reading, place a chair with its back to the window to allow sunlight to stream over your shoulder, which creates less strain on the eyes, top and bottom left.

window types

Windows are important architectural elements. The more common types of windows, such as double-hung and casement units, may act as plain backdrops for window dressings. But specialty windows are often associated with a particular architectural style. Compare a triangular window with a Palladian one, for instance. The geometric shape of a triangular window has a modern sensibility, whereas the classic Palladian-style window is considered traditional.

When selecting a treatment, it is not enough to only look at the type and style of the window. You should examine how the window relates to the space around it—its visual weight—and take into account concepts such as scale and proportion, balance, line, harmony, and rhythm. The following pages will show you how this is done.

The windows here have a strong architectural style, which may be one reason to leave them unadorned.

window classifications

If you are considering replacing a window, learn about the various types. A *fixed window* cannot be opened and is often used with an operable window. A *double-hung window* is the most common of the operable types: it has two sash that move up and down, which means that only half of the window can be completely open at one time. A *casement window* is hinged vertically to swing out. A *jalousie window* has horizontal slats, or narrow strips, of glass that are opened louver-like by a crank. A *sliding window* or *glass door* has top and bottom tracks on which the sash moves sideways.

You should also explore the various architectural styles of windows, which often influence your decor. A group of three windows with an arch over the center unit is the classical makeup of a *Palladian window*. Some variations have three arches (one large, two small) or one fanlight-style arch over the three windows. This classical window tends to visually dominate a room, so it is a logical focal point.

A *picture window* is made up of one large fixed window, often flanked by two casement or double-hung units. As the name describes, a picture window is for framing dramatic views. Like a Palladian or a picture window, a *bay window* is also composed of three parts. The difference is that the windows are set at an angle to each other, creating an alcove, or bay. A curved version of this window is called a *bow window*. A large bay with a window adds about 4 feet of extra space to a room where you can situate a chair or a small dining table.

A *clerestory window* is made of a strip of small, horizontal panes set high on a wall, near the ceiling. This window is often used in spaces where natural light is desirable but privacy must also be maintained.

There are also a variety of special small window shapes that are almost strictly decorative. These windows are used independently or in combination with the standard types. An *elliptical* or *arched window* is often placed above double-hung or fixed windows, but it can also be used alone in situations where a larger unit won't fit, such as in a dormer or a small bathroom. An *oval* (or *cameo*) *window* and a *circular window* are used in much the same way; both are sometimes located on narrow staircase landings to add light. For a more modern shape, a *triangular window* or a *trapezoidal window* is often paired with a large fixed window—a combination known as a *cathedral window*.

looking at your windows

Now that you've established the type of window you have, begin by examining how it relates to other elements in the room. Check how the window and the treatment coordinate. Look at the space itself—is there a prominent architectural style to the room? Also consider the size of the window and how it relates to the space. To get you started, here are some easy steps to follow.

OPPOSITE LEFT
This bay window, framed by a cornice and full-length drapery, adds extra footage to the room, allowing space for a table and chairs.

OPPOSITE RIGHT
Surrounded by an elaborate swag-and-jabot treatment, this traditional-style fixed-pane window looks out to a magnificent view.

ABOVE
Placed high on the wall for privacy, these three awning-style clerestory windows can be opened to let in air with the turn of a crank.

smart steps
suitability

Step 1 COMPARE THE STYLE OF YOUR WINDOW WITH THE TREATMENT YOU'RE CONSIDERING

What kind of architectural detail does the window have or lack that you can cover up or enhance? Always remember that decorating and architectural styles are linked, not necessarily in the strictest sense, but there should be a relationship between the two. Heavy brocade panels paired with formal swags will appear out of place in a country parlor. In the same way, ruffled calico curtains strike the wrong note in a room that is streamlined and contemporary.

Step 2 CONSIDER THE SIZE OF THE WINDOW

Particularly in older homes, windows are often too small, even for modest-sized rooms. Sometimes that's just because glass was expensive, so the windows were kept small. But many older houses also had no central heating at the time they were built, so the architect or builder used the same solution to avoid problems with heat loss. As homes were heated more efficiently and technologically advanced glazes were developed, window sizes grew larger. If your windows are small, you can create a more harmonious balance between the window size and the room with the right treatment and installation. For a short window, install the rod above the trim or just below the ceiling line. Hang extra-long panels, and let them puddle. On the window that isn't wide enough for the wall, extend the window treatment beyond the frame on each side of the opening.

Some windows have the opposite problem—they're so large that they overwhelm the entire space. In this case, you can tone down the scale by keeping the look simple. If a window is too tall, don't use long panels. Break up the length by dressing the top of the window with a valance or a swag that's different from the rest of the design. When windows in a room are different sizes, de-emphasize the difference with curtains that are all the same length. Don't pile on several layers, and avoid heavily patterned fabrics. (For more information on working with problem windows, see Chapter 11, "Problem Solving," page 172.)

Step 3 TAKE NOTE OF HOW A WINDOW FUNCTIONS

Does the window open inward or outward? Does it slide on a track? Where is the handle for the crank located? These small—and seemingly obvious—details can limit your window-covering choices. For instance, shutters may impede inward-opening windows. Billowing curtains may get caught in the tracks of sliding glass doors. The crank handle on jalousie windows may interfere with blinds or shades. Knowing these limitations and conditions can help you choose the most practical treatment.

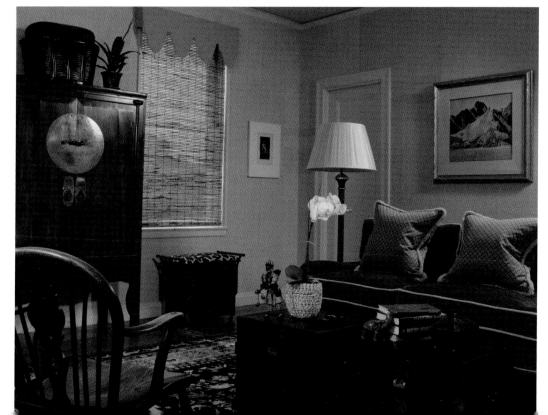

OPPOSITE
The draperies here are suspended from rings, allowing the fabric to glide effortlessly across the French doors.

ABOVE
The original wooden shutters in this nineteenth-century townhouse play an important role in the room's architecture.

LEFT
A deeply scalloped valance over a simple matchstick shade adds a decorative touch to this plain window.

scale and proportion

Dressing a window is not always as simple as hanging up attractive curtains. A window covering should be in proportion to the window and the room. If an element is not the right size—let's say, it has a rosette that's too small or an overly long valance—it throws off the entire effect of the treatment. The small rosette will be distracting rather than impressive; the long valance will make the window look squat and the room seem smaller. To plan a well-balanced window covering, there are several fundamental principles relating to space that

you should understand. These principles include scale, proportion, line, balance, harmony, and rhythm.

Scale and proportion work hand in hand. In decorating, *scale* simply refers to the size of something as it relates to the size of everything else, including people and the space itself. *Proportion* refers to the relationship of parts or objects to one another based on size—the size of the window is in proportion to the size of the room, for example. Good scale is achieved when all of the parts are proportionately correct relative to each other, as well as to the whole. If you are mixing patterns in an arrangement, for instance, you might want to balance a curtain made from a large-patterned fabric with a lining that has a medium-scale design; then use a small-print fabric for an accent, such as a border. Occasionally, a window treatment turns out to be too large or too small for its location. Careful planning and a deliberate effort will help you to avoid this and to achieve good proportion in the window covering itself, as well as its completed effect in the room. One way to test your ideas is to make a measured drawing of the window. (For more information on measuring windows, see Chapter 12, "Curtains You Can Make," page 190.) Then you can take your time and experiment with different arrangements on paper until something looks right.

ABOVE
Corner windows are integrated into the room with matching plantation shutters

RIGHT
Using the same fabric for the valance in the bay window and the adjoining draperies creates harmony between the two areas.

OPPOSITE
Draperies are a great way to soften the appearance of large windows while bringing them into scale with the furniture.

smart tip MIXING STYLES

Although it is important to keep architectural features in mind when choosing a window treatment, you can mix some styles. Classical windows don't have to wear formal swags and jabots—for example, simple panels or fabrics will let the architecture take center stage. Similarly, formal or structured treatments can enhance the architectural features of plain windows.

line

Next to consider is *line*. Simply put, line defines space. Two-dimensional space consists of flat surfaces, such as walls, floors, and windows, that are formed by intersecting lines. Adding depth, or volume, to a flat surface creates three-dimensional space—a house or a room, for example. However, lines also suggest various qualities:

■ **Vertical lines** imply strength, dignity, and formality. Imagine how impressive a pair of tall, narrow windows flanking a fireplace would look.

■ **Horizontal lines,** such as a row of clerestory windows or even a cornice across a picture window convey relaxation and security.

■ **Diagonal lines,** such as a triangular or trapezoidal window, express motion, transition, and change.

■ **Curved lines,** like those of an arched window or the shape of a swag, denote softness and sensuality.

RIGHT
The soft curved lines of this valance and drapery treatment reinforce the shape of this bow window while framing the view.

OPPOSITE
Long drapery panels seem to extend the size of the windows in this dining room. Installing the rod above the window trim adds height and draws the eye up toward the crown molding.

Windows and their coverings are a way to incorporate a variety of lines into a room's design. Most modern rooms are rectilinear. Window dressings can help relieve the repetition of squares and rectangles inherent in the architecture. Tieback draperies or fan shades can introduce a few curves and make the space more interesting.

balance, harmony, and rhythm

Balance keeps the relationships between the parts of a room natural and comfortable to the eye. For instance, two windows side by side on a wall with matching floor-length curtains will look appropriate in a room, whereas the same setting with a sill-length curtain on one window and a floor-length curtain on the other will seem awkward and out of balance. Balanced relationships can be either symmetrical or asymmetrical. A swag with two matching cascade jabots is a good example of a symmetrical design. Picture that same swag with a long jabot on just one side, and you have an example of an asymmetrical design.

Harmony is achieved by coordinating all of the elements within one scheme or motif. Matching styles, colors, and patterns are good examples.

Rhythm refers to repeated patterns, which add movement and interest. So while harmony pulls a treatment together, rhythm moves the eye. The key to creating good harmony and rhythm is balance.

Designers always suggest introducing one or two contrasting elements to a room's design. Some little surprise, such as an unexpected splash of contrasting color, can really perk up a boring design. You can apply this to a window treatment. For example, think about using a contrasting curtain liner or a band of color, beads, or fringe around the edges of a plain curtain panel to add pizzazz.

design workbook
WHAT PATTERN CAN DO

striking a balance

Large-patterned, flowered-chintz draperies make the windows the focal point in this English-country sitting room that over-looks a garden.

watch the scale

Several patterns are fine if the scale is different. Here, the size of the print on the chairs and otto-man is smaller than that on the curtains.

keep it low-key

In this small room with a low ceiling, top left, a semi-sheer curtain with a subtle pattern is just right paired with shutters on the lower half of the window.

enliven it

In a kitchen with deep, rich solid-color surfaces, left, a window valance in a perky print adds a bright note. The fabric picks up the colors of the walls and cabinets.

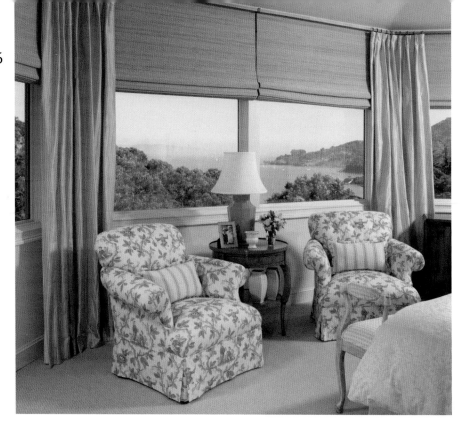

design workbook

DRESS FOR SUCCESS

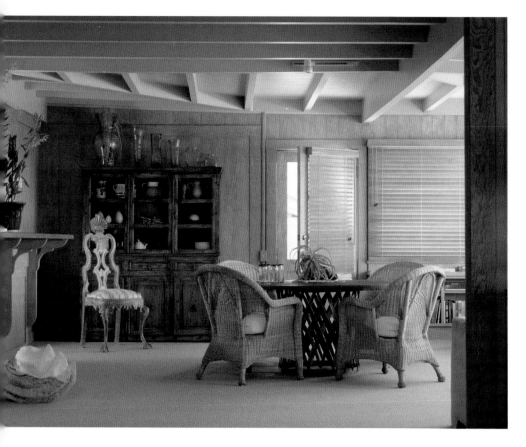

assembling balance

An easy way to create symmetry between the windows and the rest of room is to limit the overall scheme to two or three colors. (See also left.)

making a connection

By following the graceful curve of the bay windows, the lines of the built-in storage seat achieve a sense of rhythm.

worth repeating

When faced with bay windows of varying widths, top left, or a side-by-side window and door combination, bottom left, use matching materials to achieve harmony.

a good relationship

Let the architecture of the room guide you. For instance, in a clean-lined, open room, top left, use an uncomplicated window treatment.

3

planning

ASSESSING STYLE NEEDS   COLOR   PATTERN
TEXTURE   PULLING IT ALL TOGETHER   DESIGN WORKBOOK

Why does something as simple as selecting a curtain or a blind fluster an ordinarily decisive person? Perhaps it's because there are too many options. However, a good general rule for starters is to match the style of the window treatment to the style of the room.

Color, pattern, and texture are great tools for coordinating window treatments with the rest of the design elements in a room. Use them to make windows stand out or blend into the background. The most subtle of the three elements, texture, adds complexity by incorporating fabrics with matte, coarse, smooth, or glossy weaves. To try out different options, make a sample board—an efficient way to edit fabrics in different colors, patterns, and textures. Doing this will give you the confidence that what you are envisioning will accomplish your goals.

The rich fabric of the draperies installed on this bay window complements the style of this traditional room.

assessing
style needs

What do you want to achieve with your window treatment? It can enhance a space's good qualities by framing a beautiful view or incorporating color, pattern, and texture into the room. It can enliven a nondescript interior, serve as a focal point, or visually improve the room's spatial relationship. A window treatment is also an important way to establish a style. The wrong window dressing can throw off the entire decorating scheme. For example, ruffled calico curtains would look odd in a modern chrome-and-leather setting. To help you make a decision about your window-treatment needs, follow these steps.

smart steps
narrow down choices

Step 1 TAKE NOTE OF THE ROOM'S FUNCTION

In the previous two chapters, you looked at the window's function in a room—in terms of light control and privacy, as well as how its architectural style influences a space. Now look at the use of the room itself. It often dictates the type of window treatment that is needed. In a dining room—a space used mostly for entertaining—a window dressing may be chosen for its dramatic effect. A bedroom with a window facing the street may need a cover-up for privacy. To cut the glare on a desk, a study may require shades or shutters. The purpose of a room may limit your window-covering choices.

Step 2 ESTABLISH THE STYLE OF THE ROOM

Is it traditional? Contemporary? Period? Eclectic? Country? Window treatments set the tone of a room, enhancing the ambiance. Most types of treatments conjure an image of a certain style. Puddled drapery with a cornice is usually considered traditional; vertical blinds in a textured finish are more contemporary. Mixing styles can be interesting, but it takes design confidence to do it well. For instance, classic toile de Jouy curtains can be combined with rustic rattan blinds in the right setting. Window dressings in a contrasting style can be used to tone down the negative aspects of a room's design. Instead of frilly curtains, a cellular shade may keep an English-country room looking fresh. Similarly, velvet drapery can add warmth to a contem-

ABOVE LEFT
Framed against forest-green walls, the combination of bold beige-and-black-striped draperies and natural woven window shades create a distinct contemporary design statement.

OPPOSITE
By repeating the red accent color used throughout the space, the bright inset border of the crisp tailored Roman shades unifies the eclectic style of this relaxed sunroom.

porary living room, where vertical blinds may be too stark. To develop a trained eye for creating unusual combinations, look at interiors in magazines and visit designer showhouses.

Most arrangements can be successfully designed by complementing the existing decor rather than mixing styles. For a romantic bedroom, nothing beats billowing sheers or the soft silhouette of a balloon shade. The crisp lines of miniblinds enhance the simplicity of a modern living room. Gingham café curtains bring to mind country-style kitchens.

Also consider the decorating and architectural style of your home when planning your arrangement. How will the curtains or shades that you choose fit into the grand scheme? Visualize how the house will look from room to room, indoors and out. Although the window dressings in different rooms don't have to match, they should coordinate—particularly if you can see one space from another. Picture a hall that leads into a living room. The swags in the hall can be light green, picking up an accent color from the living-room curtain's floral print, for example. In this case, each space has its own style of treatment, but they are unified by a coordinating color.

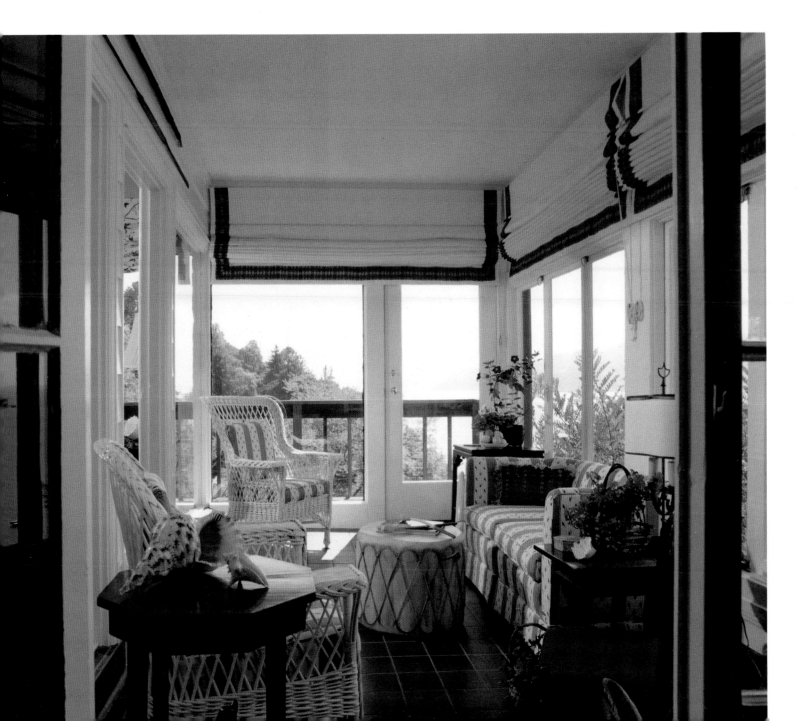

Step 3 TURN THE WINDOW INTO A FOCAL POINT, OR MAKE IT BLEND WITH THE DECOR

A window that takes center stage in the room's design should be dramatic. Strong patterns or vibrant colors are both ways to grab attention, especially if the treatment itself is fairly plain. Elaborate layers of drapery with toppers, such as swags, valances, and cornices, steal the spotlight, too. Embellishments can do the trick—think trimmings, tassels, and rosettes. A word of caution, however: when making a focal point out of an arrangement, don't let it overpower the room.

Windows that blend into a room's design create a serene ambiance. To create a low-key background, choose fabrics or colors that exactly match the walls. Neutral hues and pastels are equally soothing. Sheers add a softness and delicacy that is never intrusive.

color

You can use warm colors and cool colors effectively to manipulate the way that a window treatment is perceived. Because warm colors appear to advance, windows swathed in sunny hues seem closer together, making a room feel intimate. Conversely, cool tones and neutrals appear to recede and can be used to open up a smaller space. However, these color tricks can be employed more subtly. The less-intense version of a color will generally reduce its apparent tendency to advance or recede. Generally speaking, two contrasting colors, such as blue and orange, have the same impact as one dark color, reducing perceived space. Monochromatic schemes, on the other hand, visually enlarge space, while neutrals of similar value make window treatments retreat. Keep these effects in mind when choosing a fabric color.

TOP RIGHT
This sunny child's room decor, Inspired by the whimsical wall mural, features tieback draperies embellished with a decorative trim of bright-red stripes that coordinate with the ceiling border.

RIGHT
Draperies are a wonderful way to add pattern and color to a room. The 1950s retro-style fabric featured on this window creates a vibrant focal point in this otherwise sedate dining room.

pattern

Fabric is one of the most popular ways to add pattern to a room. Because pattern is largely a vehicle for color, the same rules that guide the selection of color effectively narrow the field when it comes to selecting a pattern or complement of patterns. The designer's old friend, scale, from Chapter 2, page 30, is the other important consideration when picking and mixing patterns.

A large-scale pattern is like a warm color in that it appears to come toward you. It can create a lively and stimulating atmosphere and generally makes a large space seem cozier. In a small area, handle a large-scale pattern with care, or it can overpower the room. That doesn't mean rule it out completely, but perhaps use it sparingly. A small-scale pattern appears to recede, making a small space seem larger. In a large room, the effect of a small pattern can be bland. From a distance it may read as a single color. If you're using small-scale pattern on window treatments in a large space, pick one with vibrant colors.

smart tip

MIXING PATTERNS

A trick for mixing patterns is to provide links of scale, motif, and color. The regularity of checks, stripes, textural looks, and geometrics, particularly if small-scale and low-contrast, tends to make them easy-to-mix "neutral" patterns. A small floral can play off a thin ticking stripe, while a cabbage-rose chintz may require a bolder stripe as a same-scale foil. Use the same or similar patterns in varying sizes, or develop a theme by focusing on floral, geometric, or ethnic prints.

BELOW
The delicate pattern and color of the draperies, cornice, and wallpaper provide a subtle contrast that pulls this nursery together.

texture

Window treatments are a natural outlet for texture. Fabric choices for draperies and curtains, as well as the fabrics and other materials available for blinds and shades, are enormous and varied. Texture can be enhanced by the way fabric is hung. Pleating, for example, creates a play of light and shadow that looks three-dimensional. You can combine layers of fabric and blinds to show off different textures.

Texture doesn't have the obvious impact on a window treatment that color and pattern wield. Its influence is subtle. But whether a material is soft or hard, smooth or rough, glossy or matte, the texture will suggest something about the overall look that color or pattern alone cannot. A variety of textures plays upon the senses and adds a layer of complexity and sophistication to a design. As with every aspect of decorating, mixing textures involves a balancing act. To give a room a distinct character, you might let one texture predominate, but the right contrast can be intriguing.

BELOW
Natural-woven material, such as that used to fabricate these tortoiseshell shades, has an appealing warmth and texture.

OPPOSITE
Sheer patterned fabrics can introduce color into a room as well as soften the look of a window without obscuring a view.

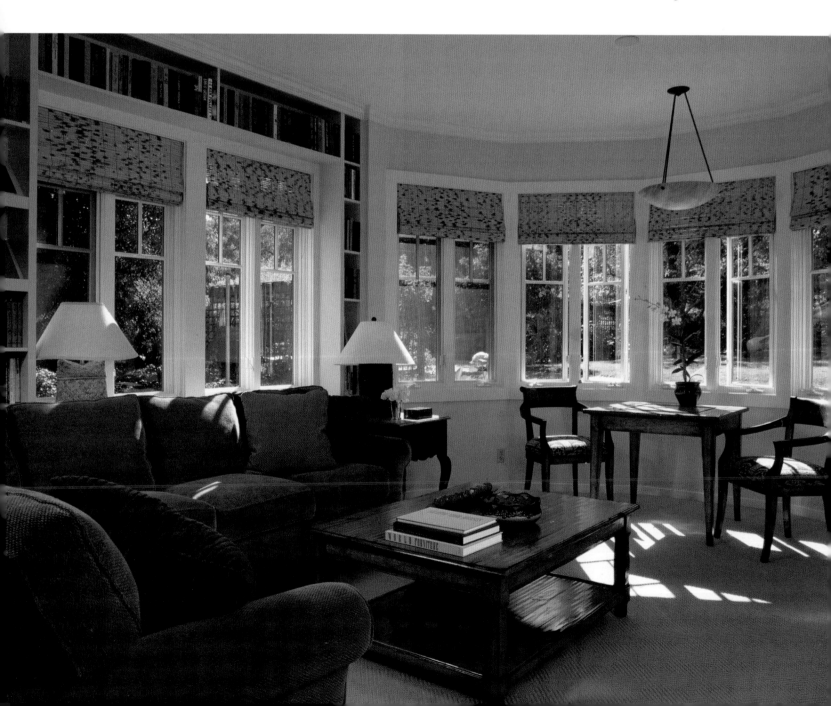

Fabrics and Textures

One of the easiest ways to introduce texture into a design is with fabric. Brocades and damasks, moirés and chenilles, tweeds and chintzes—all conjure up different looks and sensations. Coarse and matte fabrics, such as tweed, wool, tapestry, and velvet, absorb light and sound. Glossy and smooth fabrics, which range from silk and satin to chintz and taffeta, reflect light.

Before selecting a fabric, you should know that texture can affect your perception of a particular space. For example, coarse or matte fabrics on the window will make a room seem smaller and cozier than it actually is. You can use this attribute to your decorating advantage. If you have a room that is too big, too expansive, or too impersonal—such as a family room with a vaulted ceiling—tapestry draperies or wool panels will make the space feel snug. Smooth and shiny fabrics do the reverse: they make a room look larger and brighter. Small or dark areas will benefit from pale-colored silk curtains. Light reflected off the fabric will make the room look open or less stuffy.

A fabric's weave affects color, so test a sample of the material in the room. Think of how the gray color of a tweed jacket looks "heathered" and muted. On a silk shirt, however, the same gray color is shimmery and more intense—a completely different effect. Texture can also either soften or enhance a pattern. Patterns are crisp on glazed chintz but are blurred on chennille. A coarsely textured surface tones down the intensity of a color and gives the color subtle variations.

pulling it all together

You've analyzed your room's decor, and you've established whether you want the window treatment to be a focal point. Now you need to choose a color scheme, as well as mix and match fabric patterns. How do you find the best shade and pick the right pattern?

One way designers analyze the colors, patterns, and textures for a window treatment is to put together a sample board. The white, foam-cored presentation board sold in art-supply stores, measuring at least 8½ x 11 inches, is ideal for this purpose. Attach to the board with rubber cement (or tack to it with removable sticky material) any swatches of fabric, linings, and trimmings that you're considering. (If you are decorating the entire room as well as choosing treatments, it is a good idea to

include all your paint-color chips, wallpaper samples, and fabric swatches for the furnishings so that everything can be compared together.) Keep swatches and other items in the same proportion on the board as they would be on the window. For example, a fabric sample that you're considering for the curtain panels will be large, whereas the lining in an accent color for a swag will take up far less space. Add and remove things as you experiment with different looks, and be certain to look at the board in the room for which it's created at different times of the day under both natural and artificial light.

design workbook
CASUAL ELEGANCE

showing off

This classic arched window makes a beautiful design statement. Opaque draperies and jalousie slats regulate light and air. (See also bottom left.)

window jewelry

Large decorative rings, placed to visually separate the upper and lower part of the window treatment, are an important design detail. (See also top left.)

mix It up

An interesting mix of pillows provides the room with links of scale, motif, and color that result in a dramatic, yet casual space. (See also left.)

artful display

Placing a mirrored wreath on a window frame creates a pleasing symmetrical arrangement over the room's loveseat, left.

design workbook
SUMPTUOUS AND SPICY

creating a theme

The mood-changing magic of color is balanced with a unique blend of textures and materials to set the opulent theme here.

a sum of parts

A juxtaposition of elements imbues the room with an exotic spirit; the wall hanging, wallpaper, woven blinds, and fabrics add visual excitement.

customized style

Boxed cornices with an embossed pattern and decorative scrolls add finishing touches to the tieback draperies. (See also top left.)

coordinated elements

Repeating the warm colors in the elegant candle centerpiece arrangement creates a relationship among the windows, walls, and tabletop. (See also left.)

4

dollars and sense

LIFESTYLE   ASSESSING YOUR BUDGET
HIRING A PROFESSIONAL   DESIGN WORKBOOK

Decorating decisions of all kinds, including those related to selecting window treatments, should be made sensibly and in accordance with lifestyle and budget. For example, costly goblet-pleat drapery made of white slubbed silk may be an elegant choice in a living room, but not if the children play there.

When it comes to planning the budget, realistically look at how much you have to spend and how much you should spend. How much you want to spend also determines whether to order custom window treatments, buy ready-made versions, or make them yourself. The first option typically includes professional installation and cleaning. In addition, complex designs often require special skills because the window treatments are actually constructed on the window itself.

The rich fabric and tailoring of the shades complement the decorative furnishings in this formal dining room.

lifestyle

I n the previous chapter, you analyzed the room's function, noting any special needs or unusual problems that you have to address. Now you must examine your family's lifestyle. How you live influences all of your decorating decisions, and window treatments are no exception. What follows is a list of questions to help you identify these lifestyle issues. As you review these questions, don't just make mental notes of the answers. Write them down. That way, you can refer to your responses on a regular basis. This will help you stay on track all through the process.

■ **Personal Preference.** What type of interior do you prefer? Window treatments can enhance—or even change—the overall atmosphere of a room. For example, after a long day at the office, you may want to relax in a soothing interior. Soft colors set the mood. Add curtains with a blackout lining, and you can darken a bedroom at will. Do you need a more stimulating space? Fabrics in cheerful colors or sheers that let in filtered light may do the trick. Do you like the look of a window dressed in several layers, such as a swag-and-jabot valance over drapery and undercurtains? Or do you prefer just one or two elements to achieve the desired effect?

ABOVE
A window seat splashed with colorful country fabrics also features privacy-promoting shutters that match the room's relaxed style.

BELOW
Fashioned from silk taffeta, these softly gathered full-length drapery panels give the room a look of casual elegance.

OPPOSITE
The eclectic look of this living room includes the window treatment's unique mix of drapery panels and woven-blind transoms.

■ **Location.** Start by asking yourself how long you will be staying in this space. Is it a permanent family home? Are you renting? Do you have a long-term or a short-term lease?

Is this a second home, used only during specific seasons? Seasonal spaces have their own special considerations. Window treatments may need to be dirt-resistant because the house will be shut up for part of the year. They may also need to be particularly durable if many different people will be renting the house.

Where you live can be as important a consideration as how you live. For a home in the city, privacy may be a greater issue than for a home in a suburban or rural area. Even where privacy is not a factor, relatively bare windows may make some family members uncomfortable. At night, the blackness of an uncovered window can have a chilling effect, particularly for those who grew up in homes where the curtains were always drawn snug at night.

■ **External Appearances.** Does your house have a particular architectural style that is more compatible with certain types of window treatments? Because you must consider how a treatment looks from the outside of the home, this factor should play a part in your decision. For example, vertical blinds may not be appropriate for a traditional-style or historic house, yet may pair seamlessly with a house that has modern architecture. Exterior symmetry also may be important, particularly on the windows at the front of the house. What does this mean? Consider the curbside view. Treating the front windows in dramatically different styles may not have a pleasing effect on the overall exterior appearance of your house.

■ **Family Members.** The number of people in a household is another point to consider. Are you single? Newlyweds? A retired couple? A family? If you have a family, how old are the children? Are there other dependents in the house, such as an elderly parent?

Single people and couples tend to have more choices and fewer restrictions. They don't have to take into account the tastes and habits of others in the household. Plus, there is less wear and tear on all of the furnishings, including window treatments. However, if young children are frequent visitors, toddler-friendly window treatments—ones without dangling cords and puddled draperies—may be in order.

Families with young children should be realistic about their choices. Custom-made drapery in an expensive fabric, such as silk, may be too delicate or too costly to repeatedly have cleaned after assaults by grimy little hands. Attractive, washable cotton curtains, shutters with a pretty valance, or swags with short or sill-length jabots may be more practical. Also, remember that the rules for behavior that apply in your home may not be the same in the homes of your children's friends. Playing hide-and-go-seek behind the curtains can happen as quickly as your back is turned. It's simply easier to avoid potential hassles.

If you are caring for someone who is elderly or who has a disability, think about the weight of the window treatment you may be installing and its ease of operation before you make a

smart tip **PROTOCOL**

It's generally a good idea to delay any final decisions about window treatments until you have determined your wall finishes, floor coverings, and overall color scheme. This way, your room's personality will be fully developed and the treatment you choose will complement the entire room. Rods, finials, and the like can be viewed as accessories, rather than hardware, that reflect the essence of the room. In addition, if you are considering a simple treatment or relatively uncovered windows, this will give you the luxury of time to decide whether you are comfortable with the look.

final selection. Adaptations are available to make some window treatments less difficult to handle. For example, push-button mechanisms can be installed to raise and lower Roman shades or to draw heavy drapery closed. Blinds with continuous-loop cords are easier to adjust than those with pull cords.

Pets can influence your choice of treatment, too. If your dog likes to curl up in cozy places, puddled curtains that billow onto the floor are not a good idea. If your cat is indiscriminate about where he sharpens his claws, choose a style that will be out of his reach, such as shutters or sill-length curtains. And even well-behaved pets may shed. A black Labrador retriever brushing past floor-length light-colored curtains can only mean more frequent vacuuming. Shorter curtains or pet-coordinated colors may lighten your housekeeping chores.

■ **Maintenance.** Don't overlook maintenance. If a treatment requires frequent or expensive cleaning, consider whether it is right for you. For instance, if you travel often, you may not have the time to maintain formal drapery. The same is true if you have

a house full of children—you don't need another task added to your list. Low-maintenance window treatments, such as blinds that can be easily dusted and a washable valance, may require less time and expense. This is not to say that formal treatments can't be low-maintenance—a simple a pair of stationary panels may only need regular vacuuming to keep their good looks. But a multilayered window confection of double swags with cascade tails, rosettes, trimmed curtains, and sheers will take more attention. When heavy cleaning becomes necessary, you will probably have to call in a professional to dismantle the window covering, dry-clean it, and re-hang it. If your budget and lifestyle allow for these things, however, such designs have unparalleled decorative impact and may be worth the expense of the special upkeep.

Now take a look at any existing window treatments. What's in place now may be a cue to the style and function of the new drapery. Assess both the good and bad points of the existing treatments. What do you like about them? Are there any problems? What should the new treatments do that these don't?

assessing your budget

F iguring out a budget involves more than just finding out the price of a window treatment that you like. You must weigh the cost against the amount of money you have to spend and how much the treatment will take to maintain it. You also have to factor in how long you expect the treatment to last. In a rental apartment, you might want something that is flexible enough to take with you when you leave. If you've just bought your own home and intend to renovate in a few years, take those plans into account. If you're retired and this is your ultimate dream house, you may want to pull out all of the stops and go for something that you've always wanted.

OPPOSITE
Heavy, striped Roman shades blend in beautifully with the solid look of the wood trim in this traditional-style family room.

LEFT
Simple drapery panels on opposite sides of an elaborate window arch allow the architectural interest of the frame to stand out.

How a room is used may also influence your budget decisions. For example, if you entertain frequently, particularly for business purposes, then you may want to allocate a larger part of your budget to window treatments in the "public" rooms. If you are planning curtains for a baby's room, remember that what is cute for an infant's nursery may be all wrong for the room of a school-age child.

smart steps
budget wisely

Step 1 BECOME FAMILIAR WITH THE COSTS OF MATERIALS AND SERVICES

Start by visiting showrooms, custom window-treatment shops, and home centers. Also call for catalogs with ready-made examples. Compare the prices. Evaluate everything, including the fabric, the lining, and the interlining, so you are comparing apples to apples. Don't forget the details: take a look at hardware, such as holdbacks, poles, and finials, as well as tiebacks, tassels, and trimmings. If you are considering a custom treatment, talk to a design firm and find out about the fees for its services as well as the cost of installation. Because you haven't made any final decisions about the style, keep in mind that the prices you are gathering are only rough estimates. The purpose is to educate yourself about the cost of the various components so that you will be able to make realistic choices that are within your budget. If the costs seem too high, you might want to begin to explore some alternative routes, such as watching for sales or shopping the discount stores. If you are handy with a sewing machine, research some styles that are easy to make. Check out the pattern catalogs for some useful ideas. If you are considering the make-it-yourself alternative, be realistic about your capabilities. And remember to factor in your time as part of the cost.

BELOW
Used as an alternative to shades, opaque curtains placed beneath transom windows provide privacy while admitting light.

OPPOSITE
The decorative edge embellishments used on the shades and draperies in this room tie in with the trim of the pillows and sofa.

Step 2 CHOOSE A STYLE

Now that you are familiar with pricing, you can home in on the window treatment that suits your style and pocketbook. Review all of the stylistic possibilities. For a thorough guide to the choices, use Chapters 5, 6, and 7, which completely cover draperies and curtains; shades, blinds, and shutters; and cornices, valances, and swags. Now is also the time to decide what type of window treatment you plan to install: custom (through an interior designer), ready-made or semi-custom (through a retailer), or home sewn. If you don't want to go the custom-made route but are unsure about the style and color, look for an interior designer who will work with you on a consultant basis. For an hourly fee, he or she can help you narrow down the styles, fabrics, and colors that will best suit your needs and your decor.

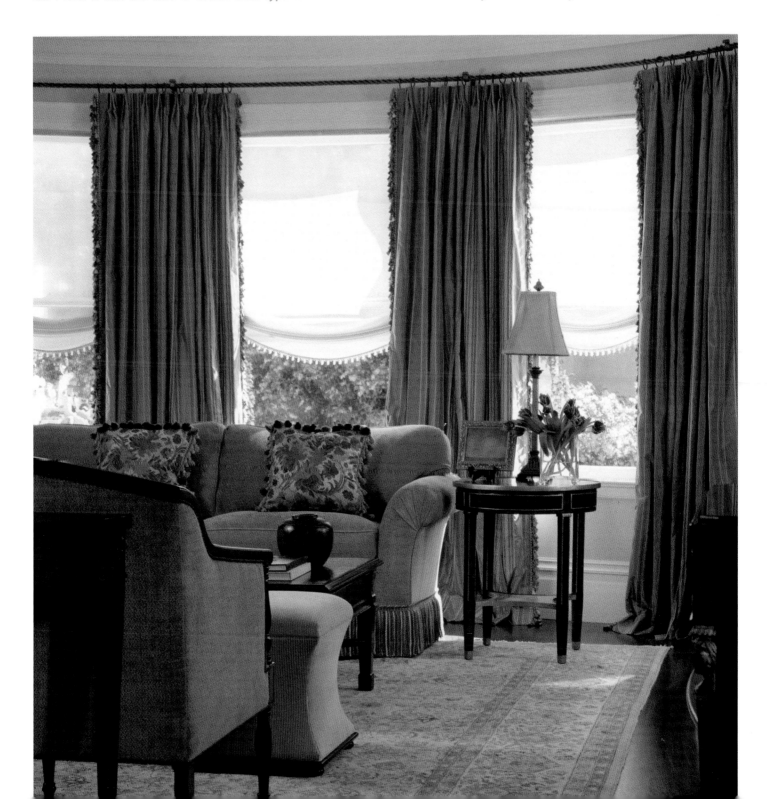

Step 3 CALCULATE THE COSTS

Add up the price of the materials (face fabric, lining, and interlining, if any), trimmings, hardware, rods, and labor. As a safety net, add 15 to 20 percent to the total to account for any hidden costs. This will give you a general idea of the expense. If the final figure is beyond your means, you have two options. First, because this is the planning stage, you can still easily make some money-saving changes. Choose a less-expensive fabric, such as a cotton instead of linen, or simplify the design: switch from labor-intensive goblet pleats to a gathered heading or opt not to use an inter-

lining. However, you may not want to compromise on the design. If so, try the second approach, which involves doing the window treatments in stages. For example, a multilayered design may have miniblinds, lined drapery, silk rope tiebacks with tassels, and a shaped cornice. Start by installing the most necessary element of the design—in this case, the miniblinds for light and privacy control. When you have the money, you can add the next layer, which consists of the drapery and the traverse rod. The last elements to be put into place are the luxurious extras—the cornice and the tasseled tiebacks.

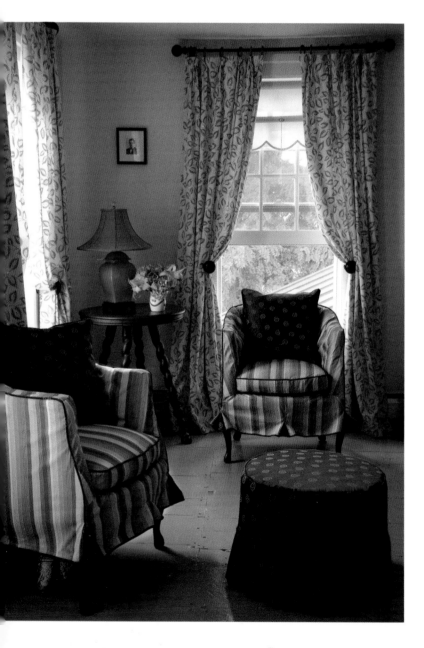

hiring a professional

If you want professional help with your window treatments, do some homework. Ask your friends and neighbors for referrals. Visit show houses; participate in house tours. These events, usually held to benefit local charities, offer you a chance to see the work of regional design talent. Check out the home-fashion articles in local magazines and newspapers. Sometimes retail establishments can recommend professionals. Search the Internet for design organizations that can make recommendations. Then, make an appointment with several professionals. They may visit your home, or you may ask to visit their workroom. Look at their portfolios. Ask for at least three references—and call and check them. It's also a good idea to contact the Better Business Bureau to make sure that there are no complaints against the professional you plan to hire.

LEFT
Dress up less-expensive, ready-made cotton draperies with decorative poles and matching holdbacks. Later, add a matching cornice or valance for a more tailored look.

OPPOSITE
A designer can help you come up with creative ways to use fabric in a room, such as using a matching pattern for the window treatment and headboard.

planning a window treatment in stages

If you're on a budget, decorate your window in stages. Stage One is a covering for privacy, such as blinds. Stage Two can be a layer of drapery panels and a traverse rod. Stage Three adds details, such as a shaped cornice and silk tiebacks with tassels.

Stage One   **Stage Two**   **Stage Three**

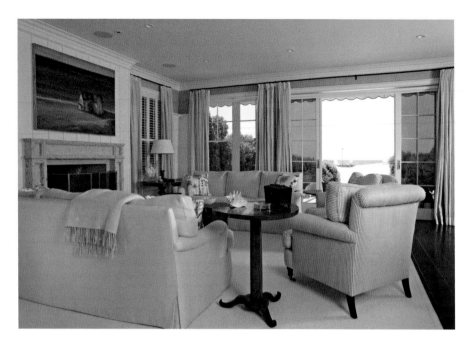

design workbook
WEEKEND RETREAT

focal point

A painting of a beach house that hangs over the mantle inspired this living room's color scheme of sky, sea, and sand.

relaxing in style

Making the most of the room's ample-size windows, left, the furnishings are arranged for relaxation and conversation.

window dressing

Floor-to-ceiling draperies add an illusion of height to the space, while painted shutters reinforce the informality of the room. (See also left.)

balancing act

Mixing textures can give a room a casual feeling, especially when you use an easy-care fabric, such as cotton, in variations of the same hue.

design workbook
UPSCALE LIVING

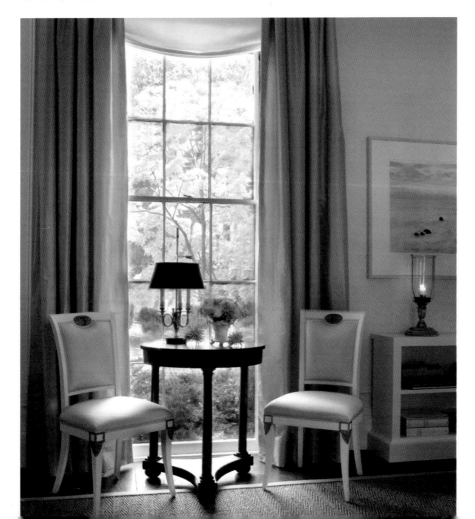

masterful mix

An interior designer can be very helpful in selecting the right fabrics to create balance and proportion in a room this size, right.

finishing touch

Floor-length draperies combined with a gently curved Roman shade soften the look of the oversized window. (See also top left.)

blending together

When dealing with a large space, use a color scheme of soft pastels on windows and other furnishings to visually unite them.

separate seating

The large window, left, acts as a perfect backdrop for this sitting area, which was designed to provide an intimate place within the living room.

5

curtains & draperies

CURTAIN BASICS WHAT'S YOUR STYLE **ROD-POCKET AND
GATHERED HEADINGS** PLEATED HEADINGS **TABBED AND TIED HEADINGS**
PIERCED AND PLAIN HEADINGS **DESIGN WORKBOOK**

Throughout this book the terms "draperies" and "curtains"
are often used interchangeably. But to some people, they have different
meanings. *Draperies* are usually pleated, lined, and floor length, with a
tailored, formal style. They are attached via hooks to a traverse rod; a
cord mechanism is used to close them. *Curtains* are normally suspended
from rods by rings, tabs, ties, or a rod-pocket casing; they have a more
casual appearance.

Whatever you call them, make note of how far you will be able to
retract the panels you have selected. Stack-back refers to how compactly
panels can be drawn back on a rod. When there is min-
imal wall space around a window or when you want to
maximize a view, the depth of the stack-back can be a
concern. Here's what else you should know.

curtain basics

Curtains encompass three basic styles: panels, cafés, and tiers. Heading variations, including pocket casings, tabs, loops, ties, grommets, and pleats, can change the personality of each style. In addition, curtains can be lined, unlined, or—for extra body and insulation—interlined. All of these elements work together to influence the ultimate appearance of your window treatment.

Types of Curtains

The basic *panel* is the most versatile and straightforward type of window dressing. It can be any length and have any type of heading. It can be hung straight, without any adornment, or tied back in one of the various positions. It looks wonderful with all sorts of hardware, including traverse rods, decorative poles with finials, curtain rings, café clips, tiebacks, and holdbacks. This multipurpose treatment can be made in a variety of fabrics with trimmings—from fringe to gimp—to reflect any decor.

A *café* curtain covers the lower half of a window. A longer version goes approximately three-quarters up the window, leaving a small section at the top of the window exposed. Café curtains are usually hung from a pole by rings, clips, tabs, ties, or a rod-pocket heading. This type of casual treatment suits cottage-style interiors. Similar to café curtains, *tiered curtains* are a team of two half curtains covering the upper and lower sections of a window. They, too, have a homey, comfortable ambiance and are hung on curtain rods.

Curtain Lengths

The curtain length influences the style of the treatment. A sill-length curtain has a casual air; drapery that falls to the floor connotes elegance. Curtain lengths also affect activity in the area near a window. Are the windows close to a breakfast table? If so, shorter curtains are less intrusive and leave clearance around the

RIGHT
Below-sill-length curtains, trimmed in a colorful print, are arranged to highlight the graceful curve of the arched window.

OPPOSITE
Hanging from a rod high above the window frame, these puddling drapery panels create an illusion of height.

table. Is there a heat source underneath the window? Curtains should never touch or block a radiator, heat vent, or heating unit. Is the treatment hung on or around a glazed door? Make sure that it doesn't block the opening and that you can open and close the door—and the curtain, if desired—easily.

Curtain lengths can camouflage problems, too. Is the window awkwardly shaped? Or is there an architectural flaw that you would like to conceal? A floor-length treatment, hung above the window frame, can help disguise the problem. In some rooms, windows may be different widths and lengths. If this is the case, plan the largest window treatment first. Dress the remaining windows in a scaled-down version of this treatment. For visual unity, install all the upper hardware at the same height.

In general, a window treatment looks best when it falls in line with the sill or floor. The most common lengths for drapery are sill, below sill, floor, and puddled. As the description implies, a *sill-length* curtain skims the windowsill. Favored for horizontal windows, it can start from the top of the window to the sill or, when café style, from the middle of the window to the sill. A curtain at this length is typically easy to operate, so it is a good choice for a window that will be opened and closed often.

The *below-sill length* falls at least 4 inches beneath the window frame so that it covers the apron, the horizontal board that runs under the sill. If the curtain is too far below the sill, however, it looks awkward and unfinished. A sill-length panel, too, can be used for café or three-quarter curtains, and it can cover up an unattractive window frame. It generally looks best on picture windows and above window seats.

curtain length

Too Short

Too Long

Correct

A *floor-length curtain* makes a strong visual statement. Make sure that the curtain is only ½ inch above the floor because, like a hem that's too high on pants, floor-length treatments that fall short can suffer the "floods." (In humid areas, however, the curtain can be an inch off the floor to allow for the rise and fall of the fabric.) If you install layered drapery, the inner curtain can be ¼ to ½ inch shorter than the outer curtain. To avoid seeing the back of the heading from the outside, add 4 inches to the curtain's length so that it hangs above the window frame. This length works well with double-hung windows, bay windows, sliding glass doors, and tall, narrow openings, such as French doors.

Puddling is the term used for a floor-length curtain with an extra allowance of fabric that is arranged into a soft pouf (the puddle) on the floor. This is a dramatic length that falls 6 to 8 inches onto the floor. (For the correct length, see the illustrations above.) Particularly appropriate for floor-to-ceiling windows, puddling has some drawbacks. A puddled curtain often needs adjustment, as it can be easily disarranged. Also, it may not be a smart choice for heavily trafficked areas or doorways, where extra fabric can block door function or cause someone to trip.

It's generally a good idea to delay any final decisions about window treatments until you have determined your wall finishes, floor coverings, and overall color scheme. This way, your room's

OPPOSITE
An extra allowance of fabric at the bottom edge of these draperies looks pretty, but be careful: puddled panels near the door opening may cause someone to trip.

ABOVE
Fan pleats add a decorative touch to these colorful sill-length panels; curtain rings allow the panels to glide easily across the pole when the homeowner wants to block harsh late-afternoon sunlight.

personality will be fully developed and the treatment you choose will complement the entire room. Rods, finials, and the like can be viewed as accessories, rather than hardware, that reflect the essence of the room. In addition, if you are considering a simple treatment or relatively uncovered windows, this will give you the luxury of time to decide whether you are comfortable with the look.

smart tip

CURTAIN WEIGHTS

A breeze can stir up a floor-length curtain, leaving it in disarray. A curtain weight can minimize the problem, plus it helps drapery to hang more smoothly. You will find two types of curtain weights: disk weights and fabric-covered weights. A disk weight is a small, round piece of lead that is inserted into the hem at each corner and each seam. To prevent it from rubbing and wearing out the fabric, insert it into a pocket made of lining fabric or muslin. A fabric-covered weight consists of links of metal encased in a fabric tube. This type, which comes in different sizes to correspond to the weight of the fabric, is attached along the hem.

High Tie   **Midway Ties**   **Center Tie**

Tieback Positions

How a curtain frames an opening is an important part of a window dressing's overall design. You can leave a curtain hanging unadorned, but by using a tieback, you can create a sculpted silhouette of fabric against a window. You can also control the amount of light that comes into the room and create a dramatic frame that enhances a view or covers an unsightly one.

Where you position the tieback affects the way a curtain hangs. The curtain can be caught back in a dramatic swoop of fabric, or it can be gently held open, revealing a colorful contrasting lining. The traditional tieback positions—high, midway, and low—are some of the most effective placements. Looping a tieback around or just below a pole, angled *high,* creates a short curve of fabric; don't use this arrangement where the curtain is moved often. A tieback positioned *midway* shouldn't fall exactly in the center; the best placement is slightly above or below the middle of the curtain. Two-thirds of the way down the curtain is

the proper place for a *low* tieback. When using this position, check that a tasseled tieback doesn't brush the floor, however.

A *center tie*—when one or two curtains are gathered at the middle so that they curve on both sides—can look impressive if it's on a bay or bow window. Use a rope tieback or, if the material is lightweight, literally knot the fabric. A *crisscross* arrangement requires two curtain rods and looks best with lightweight or sheer fabrics. When each panel is caught midway, the top halves overlap.

To create a *bishop's sleeve,* arrange two center ties at different points on a curtain (one high, one midway). Pull out the fabric above each tie to create a double tier of soft poufs. Try an *angled double* tie with a sheer undertreatment because the sinuous outline stands out against a gauzy backdrop. Slightly different from the bishop's sleeve, the two ties are arranged at the high and midway points on the panel so that the curtain swoops into graceful curves on only one side of the window.

Low Ties

Crisscrossed Ties

Angled Double Ties

smart tip HOW TO DRESS A CURTAIN

To make the folds fall evenly, train the curtains by tying them back for 48 hours or more. This is a process known as dressing the curtain and results in drapery that holds its shape and hangs well. To start, draw the drapery into the stack-back position. Fix the pleats and gaps in the heading until you are pleased with the arrangement. If the treatment is hanging below a curtain rod, position the gaps to fold toward the back; if the curtain hangs in front of the rod or pole, the gaps will fold forward. Smooth each pleat from the heading downward as far as possible. Then work from the bottom upward, gathering the pleats together. With a strip of fabric, make a loose tie just below the heading to hold the pleats in place. Tie another fabric strip midway down the curtain, smoothing the pleats as you go. Follow with a tie near the hemline. The ties should be tight enough to hold the fabric without marking it. Next, steam the curtains with a hand steamer. You may need a friend to hold the curtain while you fasten the ties. Leave the curtains undisturbed for a couple of days before removing the ties.

what's your style?

Whether you are choosing curtains for an entire house or just one room, the process is the same. You need to make three basic decisions about your treatment. Will it be formal or informal? Lined or unlined? What type of heading? Once these decisions are made, you can finalize a design.

Formal versus Informal Style

A room's window treatments are influenced by a number of elements, including the function of the space, the architectural style of the house, and the decorating preferences of the homeowner. The result is that the same windows can be treated quite differently. For example, picture a dining room with a bay window.

That type of window is often given a multilayered, floor-length window dressing—in other words, a formal window treatment. But if you prefer a more casual style, you can choose the informal look of café curtains with sill-length, tied-back side panels.

■ **A Full Formal Treatment.** Formal treatments often involve two or three layers. One layer, called the *casement curtain,* is installed inside the window's trim area. Typically it's a sheer, solid, or lace panel that lays straight or is gathered at the top. *Overdraperies,* often referred to simply as draperies, make up the second layer. Generally, they cover the window and the trim and, space permitting, extend beyond to the sides or the area above the window. The third, and optional, layer of a full formal window treatment is a *valance,* sometimes called a pelmet, which runs horizontally across the top of the window and covers the drapery or curtain heading. A hard valance, also called a *cornice* or a *lambrequin,* is usually made of wood and covered with fabric or upholstery. To some eyes, the window treatment is unfinished without this last element, but this is strictly a matter of taste. (See Chapter 7, "Top Treatments," page 108.) Luxurious,

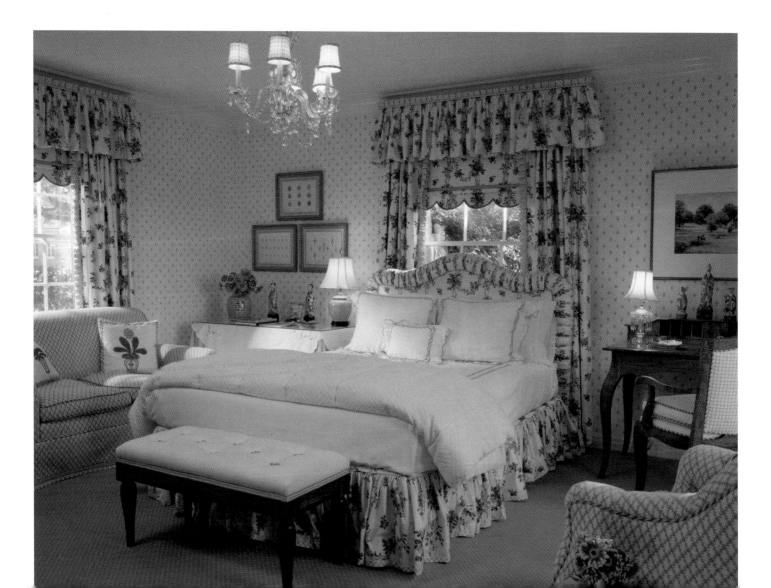

heavyweight fabrics, such as damasks, brocades, silks, tapestries, and velvets, enhance the sophistication of formal treatments. However, remember that these fabrics require professional cleaning every couple of years.

■ **An Informal Treatment.** Informal treatments may consist of one or two layers or nothing at all. Sometimes simple casement curtains look attractive in casual rooms. If only the lower half of the window needs covering, café curtains offer privacy without blocking light. Fabrics that lend themselves to an informal look include all cottons, such as chintz, ticking, toile de Jouy, linen, gingham, and muslin. Unlike the fabric that is typical of formal draperies, most of these are washable.

Lining

The style of curtains—formal or informal—often dictates whether the treatment will be lined. Other considerations include how much natural light you want in a room and how long you expect the arrangement to last.

■ **Unlined Curtains.** An *unlined* curtain diffuses daylight, but it does not exclude it. It is the simplest form of window dressing, and it is effective on its own or as an undertreatment. Because an unlined treatment lacks the extra thickness of a lining, it stacks back tightly. Choose a fabric with no right or wrong side so that it looks equally attractive from both the outside and inside of the window. Voile, lace, muslin, and sheers made of cotton or silk organza are the classic fabric choices for unlined treatments. Textured fabrics with open weaves are also suitable.

An unlined curtain filters light and provides a hazy screen from prying eyes. However, because it offers little privacy in the evening when lamps are turned on, consider pairing sheers with shades or blinds. Sunlight damage is another drawback. Without a protective lining, the fabric deteriorates quickly.

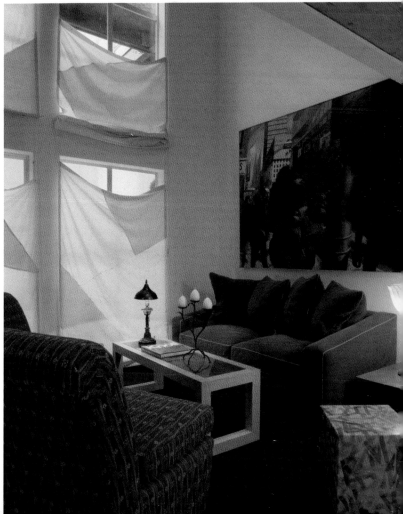

OPPOSITE
Loosely gathered fabric creates a ruffle effect above the valance's rod pocket, enhancing the feminine ambiance of this bedroom.

TOP RIGHT
A sheer curtain allows light to filter in during the day while the drapery panels provide pattern, color, and privacy when needed.

RIGHT
Fashionable yet functional sheer-linen shades highlight these oversize windows while reducing sun glare.

■ **Lined Curtains.** A *lined* curtain has body, improving its appearance by creating softer, deeper folds. A lining blocks sunlight, protecting the curtain fabric and other elements in the room from fading, particularly where there is western or southern exposure. Sunlight also adds a yellow tint to unlined fabric that may throw off your room's color scheme. A lining preserves the true color of the face fabric. Linings increase privacy, reduce outside noise, and block drafts and dust. Check for linings treated to resist rot and sun damage. Once a lining has deteriorated, the curtain can be relined or hung without the lining. To achieve the best protection possible, buy the best quality lining fabric that you can afford.

If you line one curtain in a room, do the same to the rest so that the color and drape of the curtains match. Typically, lining fabric comes in white or off-white. Although colored linings are available, be aware that light shining through a lining affects the hue of a lightweight curtain fabric. Get samples of your intended lining and curtain fabric, and then test them together at the window for color change.

Interlining

BELOW
Tiebacks on full-length, lined draperies emphasize the swooping effect at the bottom edge, softening the sliding glass patio doors.

OPPOSITE
Framing a pair of French doors and a wide window with matching drapery panels provides symmetry between all three openings.

■ **Interlinings.** If you are set on having a colored lining, consider adding an *interlining,* which is a soft, blanket-like layer of material that is sandwiched between the lining and the curtain fabric. Like a lining, it increases the insulation and light-blocking qualities of the drapery, as well as extending the life of the curtains. It also gives a professional finish to pleats by improving the drape of the fabric. A lining is usually sewn on, but it can also be attached with special double tape or pinned on with buttonholes that slip over drapery hooks. The latter allows the lining and face fabric to be cleaned separately. If you need a dark bedroom during the daytime because you work nights, try a *blackout lining,* which almost completely blocks sunlight. Other specialty linings include insulating and reflective types. These types of linings can be sewn on, but they can also be hung on a separate rod and drawn closed only when needed.

Curtain Headings

The *heading* is the top of the curtain. Headings encompass a variety of styles—from a simple casing, or fabric pocket, to complex folds that are intricately pleated. Some headings, such as tied or tabbed styles, tend to be casual, while others, such as goblet and cartridge pleats, are formal.

rod-pocket and gathered headings

A simple design is often the most effective one, which is true of rod-pocket and gathered headings. A rod-pocket heading, also known as a slot heading, is a casing (a tunnel-like pocket) created by turning the top of the curtain fabric down twice and then stitching it along the bottom fold. The rod is then slipped into the casing, and the curtain is gathered.

A rod-pocket heading can be plain, which means it lays flush against the rod, or it can have a ruffle. This ruffle is typically 2 to 4 inches deep.

Because it is difficult to reposition the fabric on the rod, choose a rod-pocket heading in situations where the curtain remains stationary. This unpretentious heading pairs well with a short, lightweight style. However, a curtain with a rod-pocket heading can also be lined and extended to the floor.

■ **Rod Sleeve.** When a rod-pocket heading is used on large openings, such as a picture window or a sliding glass door, the curtains purposely remain at the sides of the opening, leaving the rod exposed. If you don't like this look, try unifying the treatment with a rod sleeve. Used in place of a valance, a rod sleeve is a simple casing that is gathered over the rod to

Gathered Heading

Rod-Pocket Heading

Ruffled Rod-Pocket Heading

visually bridge the gap between the curtain panels. Match the style and fabric of the sleeve to the heading. If the heading has a ruffle, try a sleeve with a double ruffle—one above and one below the casing—to add detail.

Gathered Headings

A gathered heading is a soft, 2- to 4-inch ruffle created by draw-cord tape, a strip of material with strings that are pulled to create the gathers. It hangs from curtain rings or hooks. An oversized ruffle, one that is 6 inches or more, creates a cuff—a valance-like edging—on a gathered heading. (A cuff can also be a separate piece of fabric attached to the top of the curtain panel.)

■ **Bunched Heading.** A rod-pocket or a gathered heading with an over-sized ruffle can be converted into a bunched heading. This is achieved by pulling the ruffle's layers apart so that it is puffed up. (To add extra body, insert a piece of interlining into the heading.) The ruffle of a bunched heading can also be secured with stitches to create a scrunched effect. The larger the ruffle, the more pronounced this effect will be.

A gathered heading is compatible with most styles of curtains—long or short, lined or unlined. Because it is hung from curtain rings or hooks, it is easier to adjust than a rod-pocket heading. When a gathered heading is hung from curtain rings, it exposes a section of curtain rod, so pair it with hardware that has pizzazz. However, when it is hung from hooks, the traverse rod usually won't be visible.

ABOVE
With its simple rod-pocket heading, this pair of blue-and-white toile tieback curtains gives this sitting room a country-cottage look.

pleated headings

Triple-Pleat Heading

Pleats offer the greatest design impact of all the headings. These elegant arrangements have a practical purpose, too: they create supple yet disciplined folds of fabric down the curtain length.

■ **Pleat Types.** The styles for pleated headings range from the subtly sophisticated to the impressively grand. The most common is the triple pleat, also known as the French or pinched pleat, which is a trio of folds pinched (gathered and secured) together at evenly spaced intervals along the top of the curtain. Reducing the number of folds to two creates a butterfly pleat. A fan pleat is made of three or more gathered folds that rise slightly above the rod so that the fabric scallops between the fans.

A pencil pleat is the approximate width of its namesake. It is part of an uninterrupted row of pleats. Because of the simplicity of this classic heading, use pencil pleats for draperies that are meant to blend with your room's decor rather than stand out; pencil pleats often top draperies that are tucked under valances or cornices. (See Chapter 7, "Top Treatments," page 108.) By fastening pencil pleats into a latticework pattern, an elaborate smocked heading is created. A box pleat is folded so that two pleats meet, creating flat planes of fabric; although used more often for valances, box pleats can work well for draperies, particularly contemporary or tailored styles.

For a dramatic treatment, the fold of a goblet pleat is formed into a cup-like shape above a pinch. To

Fan-Pleat Heading

Pencil-Pleat Heading

Smocked Heading

Box-Pleat Heading

Goblet-Pleat Heading

Cartridge-Pleat Heading

emphasize the shapes, cording is often attached by the pinch, linking each goblet in what is called a Flemish heading. A cartridge pleat is a tubular-shaped fold without a pinched section. Both goblet and cartridge pleats are usually stuffed with a small piece of lining or batting to pad the shapes; a piece of fabric in a contrasting color can be added on top of the stuffing to emphasize the shape of the design.

■ **Stiffeners and Tapes.** To look its best, a pleated heading requires a backing made of a stiffener, such as buckram—a course cloth stiffened with glue—or a tape to keep the design in a neat formation. If the pleats are hand-folded, buckram is used to make the heading firm. Buckram comes in 4- to 6-inch widths, and it is attached by sewing or, if the fusible type, ironing.

Pleating tape, which is a strip of cotton or nylon with strings running through it, gathers the curtain fabric into the desired type of pleats when the strings are pulled. The tape ranges from 1 to 5 inches wide and has pockets for inserting the drapery hooks. Like buckram, it can be sewn or fused to the back of the heading. Tapes provide good results if you are making pencil pleats, but complex headings, such as box, triple, and goblet pleats, turn out better made by hand with a buckram backing.

Pleated curtains are often lined and interlined to add fullness to them. Because of the extra weight from the lining and interlining, hang them securely from a stationary or a traverse rod; lightweight versions can hang from curtain rings on a curtain rod.

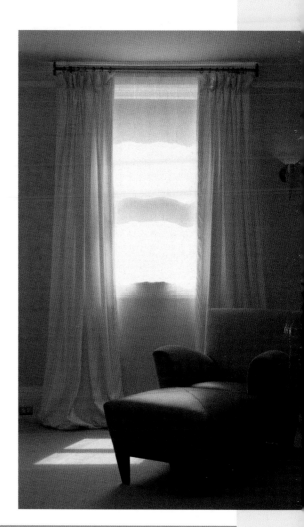

RIGHT
Cream-colored pinched-pleat draperies feature metal rings below the decorative rod, drawing the eye up to the full height of the room.

tabbed and tied headings

The casual elegance of tabbed and tied headings has recently grown in popularity. A tabbed heading is a looped piece of fabric with an exposed end (the tab) that is often adorned with a button; the button can be functional or decorative. Akin to a tabbed heading, a looped heading is a band of material without a visible tab end; it can be made of fabric, ribbon, or rope. Sometimes the fabric between the loops is scalloped, an effect favored for café curtains. A tied heading consists of two fabric strips that are tied in a bow onto a curtain rod.

Tabs, loops, and ties often look dressier when they are highlighted by fabric that contrasts with the curtain material. Another decorative accent for these headings is a cuff.

Even with a lining, these headings take up little stack-back space. However, tabbed and looped headings can be hard to adjust, so use both in stationary arrangements. By fastening a tied heading to curtain rings instead of directly onto the rod, it will move back and forth more smoothly.

Tabbed Heading

Tied Heading

Looped Heading

ABOVE
The simple panels have delicate tabs that draw attention to the bronze flowers in the decorative finial.

pierced and plain headings

Because pierced and plain headings hang from grommets or rings, they are relatively easy to move. A pierced heading is a series of either buttonholes or grommets (eyelets) that perforate the top of a curtain. The curtain rod is threaded through these openings. To vary this heading, short pieces of ribbon or cord can be pulled through each grommet and tied to the rod. A curtain with a pierced heading can be lined. To help hold the shape, use a strip of buckram to reinforce and support the heading area.

Before making a pierced heading, always check that the curtain rod fits through the grommet. If you can't find a rod that is narrow enough, consider using curtain wire, which you can hang on brackets.

A plain heading, as the name implies, is simply hemmed without pleats or tape, and then attached to curtain rings or to café clips. A lining may be added, but the extra weight may be too much for café clips. Adorn a plain heading with cuffs, borders, or bows to add definition and form. Because the rod is visible, choose eye-catching hardware, especially a design that comes with handsome finials. You might consider a pole with a decorative painted finish.

Buckram makes a plain heading lay flat; for a softer look, try interfacing, a pliable material often used in dressmaking.

RIGHT
This creative window treatment features a pierced heading with cleverly designed metal rings attached to the inside of the window frame.

Pierced Heading

Pierced Heading with Cord Tie

Plain Heading

design workbook
PERIOD CHARM

come together

Treating the French doors and side windows with the same fabric adds cohesion to the different openings.

the right mix

A peaceful palette of blue and gold is used to coordinate the various elements in this expansive Victorian-style bedroom.

luxe touch

The valance, top left, with its perfectly proportioned box-style pleats, anchors the window treatment and provides a finished look.

double duty

The combination of full-length, lined tieback draperies and Roman shades, left, serves to both preserve the view and provide privacy.

design workbook

COMFORT AND STYLE

warm tidings

Pale gold walls provide a soothing background in this bedroom. Framed by elegantly appointed windows, the bed becomes the focal point.

dressmaker details

Draped soft cornices, cinched together along the top edges, are perfectly tailored to the shape of the windows. (See also bottom right.)

room with a view

These bedroom windows, top left, are layered with tortoiseshell shades and side panels to control light while revealing the vista.

fluid movement

Lined draperies featuring a butterfly-pleat heading, far left, are attached to a bamboo pole with large metal rings, making them easy to open and close.

6

shades, blinds & shutters

**PLEATED SHADES   BASIC AND BATTEN SHADES
FESTOON SHADES   LOUVER BLINDS   HORIZONTAL AND VERTICAL BLINDS
LOUVER SHUTTERS   SHOJI SCREENS   DESIGN WORKBOOK**

Shades, blinds, and shutters offer many options for dressing a window and filtering light. Some shades completely block the light when lowered, while others diffuse the sunlight that enters the room. Some can be raised to expose almost all of the window glass, while others can be only partially raised. Blinds don't have to be raised to perform these same functions. Simply re-angling the slats does the trick. Blinds impart a more tailored look, while shutters add an architectural element, making them an intrinsic part of the home's basic character.

Any of these treatments can adorn a window as its single element, but they are still one part of the total picture and can serve to complement an existing window treatment. Curtains, valances, cornices, swags, and jabots all add layers of decorating punch to these looks.

shades

A shade is a window treatment that is raised and lowered by means of a spring mechanism or cording system. This simple definition covers a great range of styles, from flat shades to softly draped festoon shades. Today, window-shade choices go far beyond the basic vinyl roller shade and into a whole world of exciting fashion choices. But before you decide which shade will grace your window, it is important to analyze your needs and understand your options.

smart steps
know your needs

Step 1 CONSIDER LIGHT CONTROL AND PRIVACY

Are you looking for daytime control, nighttime control, or both? Do you want maximum light during the day but complete privacy at night? Will the shade have to accomplish these objectives alone, or are you pairing it with other elements that can help out? For example, you can combine a light-filtering shade that gives sun protection in the daytime with draperies that can be closed for privacy in the evening. Some roller shades and pleated shades can be installed bottom-up, covering the lower portion for all-day privacy while admitting light above.

If frequent adjustment is necessary, how easy is the operating mechanism? This may depend on the age and manual dexterity of the user. While adults find roller shades easy to adjust, small children often have problems.

Step 2 DECIDE HOW YOU WANT THE TREATMENT MOUNTED

Shades can be mounted inside or outside the window frame. Your decision can be a purely aesthetic one, or it can have some practical reasons behind it. An *inside mount* is generally used if the shade will be paired with a top treatment, such as a valance or a swag, or with a treatment that would interfere with its operation, such as drawn curtains. It is also used if the window has a particularly handsome frame that you would like to show off or if there isn't enough room outside the window frame for the operating mechanism. From a design point of view, an inside mount permits the window frame to outline the treatment, giving it visual emphasis.

An *outside mount* is used if you want to conceal the window frame, camouflage the size of the the window, or simply leave a larger expanse of window treatment on view.

OPPOSITE

Adding color and pattern to the room, these opaque Roman shades (top), block the sunlight when lowered. Sleek, contemporary-style fine-mesh shades (bottom) reduce the sun's glare while allowing the light to filter into the room.

■ Step 3 CHOOSE A SHADE STYLE

There are many different styles of shades. Some have their own intrinsic decorative character, while others are more chameleon-like, their character depending on fabric and trimming. For example, cellular shades and pleated shades (page 91) have a contemporary appearance. Because the fabric is gathered, balloon shades, cloud shades, and Austrian shades (pages 94–95) have a softer, dressmaker ambiance.

Roller shades, Roman shades, and cascade shades (pages 92–93) can easily change their personalities. When solids and geometrics are employed, they tend to have a more tailored air than when florals and laces are the chosen fabrics.

installation styles

Inside Mount

Outside Mount

Step 4 CONSIDER A HEM DESIGN

Hems can be plain or intricate, but not all shades offer the same creative hemline opportunities. Pleated shades and cellular shades do not lend themselves to fancy hems.

Roller shades, however, are the perfect canvas for a variety of hem treatments. Decoratively shaped options include scalloped, curved, geometric, and notched hems. Instead of a conventional shade pull, roller shades can have a double layer at the lower edge that is notched so that a rod can be inserted through the hemline, creating an openwork design with a stable base. These edge treatments can mirror a pattern or motif found elsewhere in the room.

Decorative trims, including fringe, cording, ruffles, lace edging, ribbon, and rickrack, can dress up the hemline of shades with cording mechanisms, such as balloon shades, cloud shades, and Austrian shades. Shades that tie, such as roll-up shades, usually have a plain hem because an embellished one would interfere with the shade's operation.

You may already have set ideas about the kind of finishing detail you want, or you may put this decision on hold until you have further explored the attributes of each individual type of shade. If you need to learn more, the information about shades on the following pages will help you reach the right decision.

Scalloped and Curved Hems

Geometric and Notched Hems

Rod and Notched Hems

Fringed, Corded, and Ruffled Hems

pleated shades

Pleated shades are a soft alternative to traditional blinds with the additional benefit of diffusing light. They come in many configurations, including ones for round, arched, and elliptical windows. Because one large shade is difficult to adjust, wide windows generally require two or more shades.

Special options include a double-cord control that allows you to move the shade in two directions—from the bottom up and from the top down (see below). Also, a track system with a split headrail makes it possible for two shades to operate on the same track. This feature is handy if you need two different types of shades, such as one for privacy or sun-filtering and one for color or style.

■ **Basic Pleated Shade.** A pleated shade is made of permanently folded paper or fabric. This type of shade stacks compactly—for instance, a 6-foot-long shade can pull back to under 3 inches. Pleats usually run as wide as 1 to $1\frac{5}{8}$ inches. Some fabric shades have a backing layer that offers high-energy efficiency, complete control of light, and privacy. Plus, they create a uniform appearance from outside the house.

■ **Cellular Shades.** A cellular shade is made of two or more layers of folded fabric, which create honeycomb-like "cells." (See above right.) Cellular shades offer a number of benefits, ranging from UV protection to privacy control to insulative qualities. Stationary versions can be made for special window shapes, such as arches and ovals.

Pleated Shade

Cellular Shade

RIGHT
Extra-wide pleated shades combine fashion and function in this contemporary foyer, offering crisp tailoring mixed with UV protection, privacy, and insulation.

basic and batten shades

Basic and batten shades are those that, when lowered, present a smooth surface against the window. This category includes roller shades (firm shades that can be made from fabric or vinyl), roll-up shades, fan shades, cascade shades (soft, stationary shades that have a distinctive draped effect when they are raised), and Roman shades (which are relatively firm and usually made from fabric).

■ **Roller Shade.** Roller shades can be purely functional or highly decorative. They're particularly good for small windows where you want to take advantage of the light. Generally, a roller shade is operated by a spring mechanism that is activated by tugging at the lower edge. This lower edge can be plain or embellished in any number of ways. A decorative pull (handle) can also be added to prevent wear on the lower edge of the shade.

The shade itself is made from vinyl or a tightly woven fabric. The fabric is either laminated (glued) to a backing or treated with a stiffening agent to give it firmer body. You can purchase roller shades in a variety of colors (usually neutrals and pastels), textures, and finishes. You can also have shades custom-made to match or complement fabric used elsewhere in the room. And you can make your own shades, using your own fabric. Kits are available that contain a roller with a built-in winding mechanism, brackets, wood batten (bottom slat), and hardware. To stiffen the fabric, treat it first with a special liquid or spray stiffener, or apply an iron-on backing designed specifically for shades.

Roll-Up Shade

Fan Shade

LEFT
A sheer roll-up shade that diffuses light during the day is combined with a roller shade that can be lowered at night.

OPPOSITE
This cascade shade features a scooped shape along the bottom edge that creates a neat but softened look.

Cascade Shade

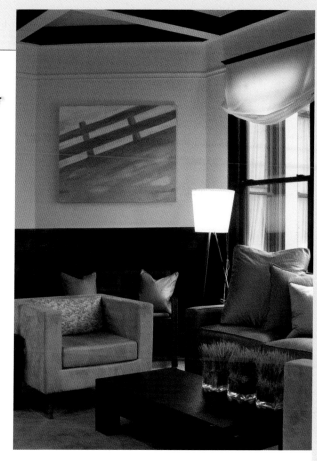

■ **Roll-Up Shade.** A roll-up shade, sometimes called a tied shade, is stationary. If it hangs from a pole or a shelf mounted outside the window frame, there should be enough room on the wall on both sides of the window to install the brackets. Once the shade is hung, the bottom part is rolled up to the desired position and secured with ties. The shade can be designed so that the lower edge folds into a soft swag when tied, or the lower edge can be reinforced with a batten. It needs a fabric that isn't too heavy but will stay in place, such as a silk taffeta. Strong, bold patterns work well on this particular type of shade. For visual punch, use contrasting ties.

■ **Cascade Shade.** Similar to a roll-up shade, a cascade shade usually has two sets of rings and cords sewn in a vertical arrangement onto the back of the shade. When the cords are pulled up, the sides swing in, giving it a scooped shape. To stabilize the shade, a rod can be inserted along the lower edge, centered between the rings. This shade is usually unlined.

■ **Fan Shade.** Another type of stationary shade, a fan shade, has a single set of rings and cords that raises the center of the shade. This causes the sides to swing down, creating fan-shaped folds. Two battens, inserted along the hemline and meeting at the center, stabilize the shape. It looks best in plain and small-patterned fabrics, and it has a more formal appearance than other fabric shades.

■ **Roman Shade.** Unlike roll-up and fan shades, a Roman shade is a fabric shade that can be raised or lowered at will. When raised, it folds up evenly at regular intervals. These folds are created by a system of rings, cords, and precisely spaced horizontal battens. It is not hung on a rod. Instead, a Roman shade is mounted on a board that is attached inside the window frame or on the wall above the frame to let in full light.

This versatile treatment can be lined and insulated or made from a single layer of sheer fabric. A Roman shade can be designed so that it is smooth when lowered or has small, overlapping folds. A fold should never be more than 8 inches wide because the shade will not pull up evenly and the battens will bend. For wide windows, use multiple shades.

festoon shades

Festoon shades are gathered fabric shades that add softness and femininity to a room. They are designed to be raised or lowered by means of a ring- and-cord system that is attached to the back of the shade. When extended full length, festoons look like a gathered and scalloped curtain. When drawn up, they get fuller, poufed-up edges.

The amount of fullness—or pouf—can be controlled by the placement of the cords and rings. Wide spaces between them means shallower scallops. Narrower spaces mean deeper scallops. It is not necessary for all the scallops to be the same width. For example, a festoon could have a wide scallop in the center and narrow ones at the ends.

■ **Balloon Shade.** A balloon shade is gathered in scallops across the width of the shade and is raised in soft folds by a cording system. Although it can be designed with one scoop, a balloon shade is typically three to four scallops wide and has an inverted-pleat heading. The result is a slightly tailored shade with ruching that falls only along the scallops.

When lowered to floor or sill level, a balloon shade looks like a full-length curtain. However, if you prefer the scalloped shape, increase the length of the fabric so that the ruching remains even when the shade is completely lowered. To accent the shape of the hem, add ruffles or fringe. (Smaller details, such as cording, won't show up.) Another hem option is called skirting. Leaving off the bottom rings creates a flat panel, over which the scallops fall.

Balloon Shade

Tailed Balloon Shade

ABOVE
These richly colored, opulent red balloon shades are finished with a decorative fringe trim that accents the shape of the hem.

Choose fabrics in solid colors or simple patterns for balloon shades. Stripes, checks, plaids, miniprints, and small-scale florals work well, but bolder patterns may look excessive and may be distorted by the ruching.

■ **Tailed Balloon Shade.** By omitting the side cords on a balloon shade, a tail is created. Tails can be just a few inches long or dramatic drops that are double the width of the scallop. Long tails look best with shades that are only one or two scallops wide. Shorter tails are better when there are multiple scoops. A contrast binding along the lower edge or sides accentuates the shape.

■ **Cloud Shade.** When a balloon shade has a gathered or pleated heading, such as a pencil pleat, it is often referred to as a cloud shade. A cloud shade has a scalloped hem and exuberant ruching, which results in a very feminine treatment. The lower edge is usually left plain or trimmed with a deep ruffle; a narrow trim would simply get lost in the billowy edge.

■ **Austrian Shade.** The full fabric length is at least double the drop in an Austrian shade. As a result, even when the shade is completely lowered, horizontal scallops remain. Often made from a sheer or lacy fabric, it looks great alone or as an undercurtain for heavy draperies.

RIGHT
This tailed balloon shade has a double-cord system that allows you to position the fabric at different heights.

Skirted Balloon Shade

Cloud Shade

blinds

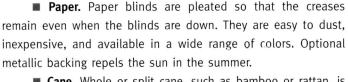

Blinds encompass a group of hard window treatments composed of movable slats. Blinds can be raised and lowered; many versions can also be opened and closed to permit varying degrees of light to enter the room. They have a linear quality that is compatible with tailored and contemporary interiors. For a traditional decor, blinds are usually combined with curtains for a softening effect.

Materials

Slats are made from a variety of materials that are generally firm or rigid in nature. These slats are strung together so that they can be rolled up, usually on a spring mechanism, or pulled up with a cord.

■ **Paper.** Paper blinds are pleated so that the creases remain even when the blinds are down. They are easy to dust, inexpensive, and available in a wide range of colors. Optional metallic backing repels the sun in the summer.

■ **Cane.** Whole or split cane, such as bamboo or rattan, is used for blinds that roll up or fold into pleats. Small spaces between the slats let through some light, which makes blinds made from this material translucent from inside and outside the room.

■ **Metal.** Aluminum alloy is the traditional material for Venetian blinds, which have slats that are slightly curved. They come in a variety of widths, from $\frac{1}{2}$ to 2 inches wide, and can be custom-fit for special-shaped windows or cut to fit around air conditioners.

■ **Wood.** For Venetian blinds, wooden slats are 1 to 2 inches wide. Tapes or thin cords control the movement. Adjusting the angles of the slats controls the amount of light. The slats can be stained or painted. They offer a natural look, durability, and insulating properties. Woven cloth tapes are available with wood-slat blinds in coordinating or contrasting colors. Narrow strips of wood are also used for woven blinds.

■ **Plastic or Vinyl.** Plastic or vinyl 1-inch slats function the same as wood or aluminum versions but are less expensive. Aside from a range of colors, options include high-gloss and pearlized finishes.

■ **Fabric.** Stiffened, textured fabric is often used for vertical blinds. For specialty blinds, fabric slats form an interior layer that is sandwiched between two sheer facings. The sheer fabric softens the hard lines of traditional blinds. Plus, when open, it lets light filter into the room and provides some degree of privacy.

LEFT
In this window treatment, colorful vinyl blinds are paired with subtle decorative valances to coordinate the windows and the soft canopy of the bed.

woven blinds

As a category, woven blinds tend to be informal in style and contribute to the casual, outdoor feeling of a room. They are good for family rooms, sunrooms, and porches, but they also show up in kitchens and bathrooms. Woven blinds come in standard sizes and are composed of inexpensive materials, making them the most reasonably priced option when compared with other types of blinds.

To create these blinds, narrow horizontal slats are woven together using strips of cotton twine. Woven blinds may be mounted inside the window with screw-and-eye hangers. A pulley system pulls the blinds up. They can be fixed at any level by winding the cord around a cleat that is attached to the wall. Use them alone or with a top treatment.

■ **Matchstick Blinds.** Made from very thin strips of natural fibers, matchstick blinds are usually cane or basswood. A matchstick blind can be stained, painted, or left natural. It filters the light during the day, but because there are spaces between the slats, it does not offer complete privacy during the day or night.

■ **Plastic Blinds.** Similar to a matchstick blind, a plastic blind is constructed from narrow plastic slats, called quills, with closely spaced strips of twine. It comes in white and a wide range of colors. Plastic blinds are somewhat less bulky than matchstick blinds.

Matchstick Blind

Plastic Blind

RIGHT
Matchstick blinds enhance the exotic ambiance of this living room.

horizontal and vertical blinds

Traditional slatted blinds come in a wide variety of materials and finishes. Used alone, they have a linear, almost industrial quality that works well in a contemporary setting. However, it is easy to warm up blinds by pairing them with curtains or any of the fabric top treatments.

■ **Venetian Blind.** Usually made from aluminum, the venetian blind consists of a series of 1-, 2-, or 3-inch-wide horizontal slats held together by cords and twill tapes. The slats can be raised, lowered, or angled to control light. It comes in many colors and finishes, including anti-static, metallic, pearl, suede, and a perforated finish that permits light to enter even when the blind is closed.

■ **Wood-Slat Blind.** A Venetian blind constructed from wood is called a wood-slat blind. The finish can be natural, stained, or painted. Because wood slats are thicker, wood blinds have a deeper stack than that of aluminum when pulled up. When down, this blind is reminiscent of shutters, particularly when the slats are in the closed position.

■ **Miniblind.** Narrow, ¹/₂-inch-wide aluminum or PVC Venetian blinds are called miniblinds. They are particularly popular because when the blind is lowered and fully open, the slats are almost invisible. They come in a wide range of colors to match almost any decor. The 1-inch-wide blinds are also sometimes referred to as miniblinds.

■ **Vertical Blind.** Although vertical blinds are especially popular in offices, they are equally prevalent at home in a contemporary residential setting. They are installed on a track across the top of the window so that they can be drawn closed, just like draperies. Remote-control mechanisms are available so that they don't have to be closed by hand. The slats can be linked together at the bottom by a metal chain or left hanging free. The slats are commonly made from wood, synthetic flexible material, or stiffened fabric. Special track systems are available for bow, bay, and angled windows.

■ **Window Shading.** A special type of blind, called a window shading, features soft fabric slats inserted between two layers of sheer fabric, allowing daylight to filter through the open slats. Window shadings are available in horizontal and vertical styles. The fabric on the horizontal blinds lies flat; the vertical version falls in soft folds like pleated drapery. This can be an alternative to a vertical blind if you prefer the look of something softer than a blind but more structured than a lightweight curtain.

RIGHT
Movable slats, a feature of Venetian blinds, let you play with natural light.

OPPOSITE
Vertical blinds placed below this large circular window create visual balance.

Wood-Slat Blind

Vertical Blind

Miniblind

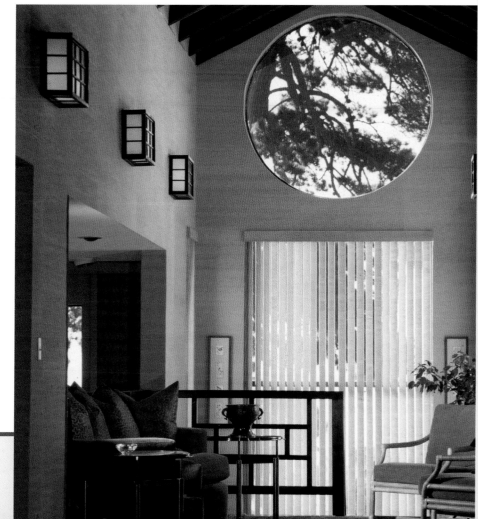

shutters

Shutters conjure images of cozy interiors that envelop you in warmth and comfort. They can be installed inside the window frame on a mounting strip or outside the window opening in a frame of their own. Depending on the size of the window, they can be installed as a single shutter that swings open to one side of the window, as a pair that opens in the center, or as four or more panels that are hinged together and split at the center.

Shutters offer various options for privacy. Because they are good companions to almost any top treatment, they can be installed to cover the lower half of the window only. They are also a good buffer against noise, which makes them popular for street-level rooms in urban areas. When a window has two or more sets of shutters, a divider rail can be installed so that the top half can open separately from the bottom.

As a general rule, use the minimum number of panels possible to achieve the desired effect. More panels mean that more of the window is covered by the frames. Fewer panels will give you the most unobstructed view and allow you to control the light better.

Louvers are the vertical and horizontal slats that give shutters their character. Standard louver widths are $1\frac{1}{4}$, $1\frac{3}{4}$, $2\frac{1}{2}$, $3\frac{1}{2}$, and $4\frac{1}{2}$ inches. Wider louvers allow more sunlight into a room; narrow slats provide more screening.

BELOW
These vinyl shutters are designed with adjustable louvers to control the amount of sunlight in the room.

OPPOSITE
Staining the three wood shutters to match the cabinets enhances the rustic ambiance of this French country-style kitchen.

Materials

There are two materials that are used to make louvered and paneled shutters: wood and vinyl polymer.

■ **Wood.** Shutters are usually made of pine. Unfinished wood shutters can be stained or painted any color; some styles are available prepainted in standard and custom colors. Wood shutters are a durable investment that enhances a home's value.

■ **Vinyl.** Vinyl polymer solves the problem presented by wood: warping in bathrooms and other areas where there is steam and moisture. This material also wipes clean easily.

smart tip SHUTTERS

For the maximum amount of light coming through shutters, use the largest panel possible on the window. Make sure the shutters have the same number of louvers per panel so that all of the windows in the room look unified. However, don't choose a panel that is over 48 inches high, because the shutter becomes unwieldy. Also, any window that is wider than 96 inches requires extra support framing.

louver shutters

There are three basic types of louver shutters: plantation, vertical, and café. If these don't suit your exact needs, be aware that shutters can be custom-fitted to specialty shaped windows, such as arches. With most of these configurations, louvers will not be movable.

■ **Plantation Shutter.** A shutter with a generous proportion is called a plantation shutter. For this style, the louvers are generally $2\frac{1}{2}$ to $4\frac{1}{2}$ inches wide and are set into panels that are 15 to 36 inches wide. Plantation shutters are frequently used in multiple sets, covering the entire window from top to bottom. These attractive shutters are also frequently used alone without any other window treatment. They can be installed as sliding pan-

els, too. This is an arrangement that is suited to floor-length windows.

■ **Vertical-Louver Shutter.** A vertical-louver shutter is a traditional type with louvers generally $1\frac{1}{4}$ inches wide and set in panels 8 to 12 inches wide. If you wish to mount it inside the window frame, you need a 2-inch clearance between the face of the window and the back of the shutter so that the louvers can open freely. If the distance is less than 2 inches, an outside mount will be required.

■ **Café Shutter.** Café refers to the type of installation, rather than the style of the shutter. Like a café curtain, it is installed to cover half of the window. It can cover the lower half only, or a set can be double hung to cover the upper and lower halves of a window.

Café Shutters

Vertical-Louver Shutters

LEFT
A perfect choice for this bathroom window, café shutters provide a combination of privacy, light, and ventilation.

more shutter styles

Strictly speaking, shutters can be any type of movable window covering that is set into a frame—a panel shutter is the most classic example of this. A fabric-insert shutter and a Shoji screen are other variations. No light passes through a closed panel shutter. However, a fabric-insert shutter or a Shoji screen diffuses light when closed.

■ **Panel Shutter.** A panel shutter consists of solid pieces of wood or interlocking strips of wood. It usually has some type of decoration, such as raised moldings.

■ **Fabric-Insert Shutter.** Consisting of panels of gathered fabric set into a wood frame, a fabric-insert shutter can be used to create a more colorful look than that of traditional shutters. The fabric can be printed or plain, solid or lace; it can be selected to match the wallpaper or to repeat a fabric used elsewhere in the room. The best choices are light- to medium-weight fabrics that gather easily. An unlined fabric panel can be damaged by sun, so choose a sun-resistant fabric.

■ **Shoji Screen.** A shoji screen consists of a translucent panel set into a delicate wood frame. It usually slides open on a track, but it can also be hinged to work like a shutter. Often used as doors, shoji screens are also appropriate for windows. In traditional Japanese homes, the panels were originally made from rice paper. Today, panels are made from durable synthetic materials. This covering is compatible with both contemporary and Asian decor.

RIGHT
The shoji screen is an attractive minimalist treatment for windows or patio doors.

Shoji Screen

design workbook
ALTERNATE VIEWS

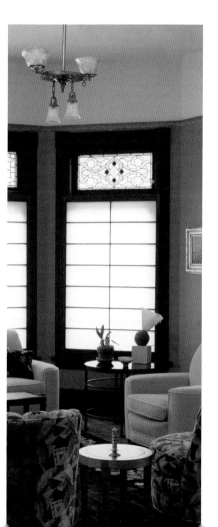

focal point

The use of sleek metallic panels, vertical blinds, or framed shoji-style panels adds architectural interest to a modern setting (See also left).

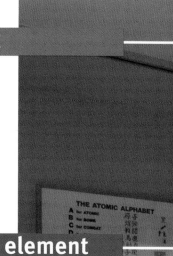

decorative element

The decorative addition of a wide teakwood cornice extending across one side of the room provides a cohesive look between the wall and window.

surrounding space

Vertical blinds provide treatment for windows, far left, or patio doors while allowing the room's architecture to remain on view.

as you like it

Available in a wide variety of custom designs, shoji screens, left, are a versatile addition that can be used in both modern or traditional settings. (See also top left.)

design workbook
NICE AND NEAT

elements of design

Hobbled-style Roman shades have folds that stay put when raised or lowered. Flat shades fold at the edge. (See also top and bottom left.)

center of attention

Roman shades, mounted inside the frame, draw special attention to the paired windows while offering an uninterrupted view of the vista outside.

stripe it rich

Bold awning-striped fabric on Roman shades, top left, used to cover the patio doors, gives this beach-house living room a carefree summer look.

perfect match

Two separate elements, a window and a patio door leading to a balcony, are visually united with the addition of brightly colored matching Roman shades, left.

7

top treatments

SWAGS AND JABOTS   STRUCTURED SWAGS   SCARF SWAGS   VALANCES
BALLOON VALANCES   PLEATED VALANCES   TABBED VALANCES   GATHERED
VALANCES   CORNICES   SHAPED CORNICES   BOX CORNICES
LAMBREQUINS   DESIGN WORKBOOK

Originally, top treatments were more practical than decorative, providing an added layer of insulation over drafty windows. As more fabrics and dyes became available, cornices, valances, and swags became stylish. Today, ruffled valances soften the look of hard treatments; padded box cornices complement the tailored look of vertical blinds; and ornate swags add drama to a plain paneled curtain. Used alone, top treatments can be fashionable without compromising the view or natural lighting.

In addition to hiding hardware and camouflaging imperfect curtain headings, top treatments can improve the appearance of poorly proportioned windows. With the exception of a cornice, you can position any top treatment inside or outside of the window frame. Make it distinctive by adding complementary colors and special trimmings.

An upholstered box valance, detailed with rope-style piping and decorative knots, conceals the hardware.

swags
and jabots

Swags and jabots are purely decorative window treatments. We tend to think of them as gracing tall windows in stately country homes and elegant town houses, but they can be a beautiful addition to any room. Heavy fabrics, such as brocades and velvets, and elaborate trimmings are in keeping with their original formality. However, making them with lighter-weight fabrics and simpler trimmings, as well as mating them with shutters or blinds, produces a less-formal look.

Swags are the scallop-like shapes that extend across the top of the window. *Jabots* are the tails. They can be pleated or softly shaped vertical panels with symmetrical or asymmetrical hemlines that flank a swag.

smart steps
plan your top treatment

Step 1 CHOOSE A SYMMETRICAL OR ASYMMETRICAL ARRANGEMENT

In a symmetrical arrangement, the window treatment is the same on both sides of an imagined or real centerline. An example of a symmetrical arrangement is a series of three swags with matching jabots framing a picture window. The middle swag is positioned so that its center is exactly at the center of the window; one swag and one jabot flank it on each side. Because a symmetrical treatment appears formal, it looks appropriate in a traditional setting.

An asymmetrical arrangement refers to the balance between different-size elements of a window treatment as a result of placement. For instance, a circular window can be dressed with a swag that has a long jabot (tail) on one side and a short one on the other. As long as the scale of the treatment is correct, the results will be visually pleasing.

Because an asymmetrical arrangement appears informal, it suits a casual, contemporary interior. But it can also work well in a traditional setting. Imagine a wall with a fireplace and two windows that are equal in size and distance from the fireplace. Each window could have a short jabot on its inside edge and a longer one on its outside edge. Individually, each window arrangement is asymmetrical, but because they are mirror images of each other, the overall result appears formal and symmetrical.

Step 2 DETERMINE THE NUMBER OF SWAGS THAT YOUR WINDOW NEEDS

The size of the window affects how many swags are needed. As a general guideline, swags should be no more than 40 inches wide. The depth (or drop) of each swag generally ranges from 12 to 20 inches, depending on the height of the window.

Narrow windows look better with one or two swags. More than two will look crowded on a small window. The swags should overlap slightly. If the swags are paired with a curtain or a blind, they should overlap enough to conceal the headings underneath.

Wide windows require multiple swags to match their generous proportions. Generally, use an uneven number of swags so that you can position one full swag to fall in the center of the window.

To help you decide how many swags you need, draw your window to scale on a piece of paper. Using tissue-paper overlays, sketch different arrangements. When you find a pleasing one, drape lengths of string or cloth measuring tape across the top of your window to mimic the desired effect.

Step 3 DECIDE BETWEEN A FORMAL OR A CASUAL STYLE

This depends on several factors: the room's decor, the look you want to achieve, and the style of your curtains. Formal versions of swags and jabots are mounted on a board that is attached to the wall or the window frame. They are usually made from mid- to heavyweight fabrics, such as velvet, brocade, or satin, and they are lined. Trimmings, including tassels and braids, can be opulent. Formal swags and jabots are usually paired with curtains and, sometimes, sheer inner panels. Informal versions tend to be made from mid- to lightweight fabrics, such as chintz, linen, or voile. They often serve as top treatments for blinds and shutters. Informal swags and jabots may be mounted on a board but can also be hung from rods. Trimmings are applied with a light touch. Some informal swags are unlined and resemble scarves casually tossed over a pole.

OPPOSITE
An artfully arranged swag, placed high over the bathroom window, provides a decorative focal point while optimizing the view.

BELOW
To add contrast to this tailored treatment, gingham fabric was used on the cornice and on the underside of the jabots.

structured swags

Although a swag-and-jabot arrangement looks as though it is made from one piece of material, each element is actually a series of separate sections. A swag can have a deep or a shallow drop. The deeper the drop, the fuller the folds.

A fan swag, which has folds that radiate out from the top center, is a variation of the traditional swag. Swags and jabots can also be hung on a rod with rings to form an apron-like effect over side curtains. Another variation foregoes the mounting board in favor of hidden hardware installed at the top of each jabot. This creates

a crown-like design above a French door in rooms where there are unusually high ceilings, or it can enhance the illusion of a taller window.

Jabots are the tails of fabric that complement the swags. There is generally a jabot at each end of the treatment. However, for more visual interest, the treatment can also be designed with alternating swags and jabots. You can plan the jabot to lie under or over the ends of the swag.

Jabots are usually lined because the added weight helps them to hang better. If the underside is visible, a contrast lining is often used to accentuate the shape of the design.

The most common jabot style is the cascade, an asymmetrical tail that is formed by fan-folding the fabric. When all the folds are arranged exactly on top of each other, the jabot falls in a narrow, stacked pattern. When the folds are stag-

gered, the jabot is wider and the hemline undulates upwards. The other common asymmetrical tail is the spiral—a corkscrew-like arrangement. Asymmetrical jabots are used in mirror-image at the ends of the treatment.

Symmetrical jabot styles include the fluted jabot, an open tube that curls to the underside, and the pipe jabot, a closed tube with a pointed hem. Symmetrical jabots are used at the center of the window, between the swags. They also can be used at each end in place of an asymmetrical tail.

Trimmings pair naturally with swags and jabots. The deep scoops of the swags and the undulating edges of the jabots often feature bullion and pom-pom fringe, cording, and ribbon borders. Rosettes, choux (ruched rosettes), Maltese crosses, and tassels can be added at the point where the swag is attached to the jabot.

Swag on Curtain Rings

Fan Swag

Triple Swag and Cascade Jabot

Swag on Curtain Hold Backs

RIGHT
Red-and-white-striped trim adds a festive touch to this blue-and-white treatment. The swag valance does not hamper the use of the French doors.

Cascade Jabot

Spiral

Fluted Jabot

Pipe Jabot

scarf swags

Scarf swags are a more relaxed interpretation of the swag-and-jabot treatment. They can be short, meaning sill length or shorter, or long, to the floor or gracefully puddling. Generally, a scarf treatment is created from one long piece of fabric. Lightweight fabrics with no right or wrong side, such as batiste, voile, lace, linen, and lawn, are good choices because they will fall into the soft folds that make scarf swags attractive yet informal.

Scarf treatments can be wrapped over poles; suspended from brackets, hold backs, or rings; or tacked up with decorative hardware. Special brackets are also available to secure the fabric into various swag, tail, and rosette formations while remaining completely hidden from sight.

Scarf swags that are sill-length or shorter require some care to establish pleasing proportions. If the scarf is used alone, the tails should extend at least one-third of the way down the window. Otherwise, the end product tends to look a bit skimpy. Short scarves can also be installed over floor-length curtains to add drama to the window.

When a floor-length scarf is arranged to hang over a curtain rod, the effect is called a "draped pole." However, it can be tricky to get the hemline right because there is so much fabric. To solve the problem, let the bottom of the fabric puddle on the floor. Because it is heavy, a long scarf also requires more support than a short treatment. An asymmetrical style can be an interesting counterpoint to an odd-shape window.

Crisscrossed Draped Pole

Wrapped Draped Pole

Scarf Swag on Brackets

Asymmetrical Draped Swag

Double Scarf Swag

OPPOSITE
Matching minimalist swags provide a unifying theme in a room designed with various-size window and door openings.

TOP RIGHT
Embellished with a choux at each corner, this large window is framed in a floor-length scarf swag that ends in a puddle.

valances

Valance is an all-encompassing term used for a range of treatments that are designed to be purely decorative. It is a soft fabric treatment that is usually draped, gathered, or folded. It covers no more than the upper third of the window glass, and generally covers much less. A valance can take many forms—from simple bands of fabric to elaborate arrangements with gathers and pleats. It can accompany curtains or stand alone.

While a valance does not contribute to privacy or light-blockage (except minimally), it does provide a way to add color and interest to a window, visually balance curtains or shutters below, and add another layer of decoration that can be enhanced by cords, gathers, pleats, and trim. From a practical point of view, it hides any unattractive hardware that belongs to underneath treatments, such as plain curtain rods and shade rollers. It also softens hard treatments, such as wood or metal blinds.

■ **Proper Proportions.** The valance should be in proportion to the window. This means that it should not be so long that it blocks the light or so short that it looks like a skimpy afterthought on the window. Longer windows mean longer valances. Valances are generally between 10 and 16 inches long, including the heading and any trim at the lower edge. Valances that involve generous swoops and folds of fabric, such as some variations of the balloon valance, may be a little longer to accommodate the abundance of fabric. Valance tails should fall one-third of the way down the window.

Several other factors will influence the proportions of your valance. For an outside mount, the valance should be longer so that it extends to a pleasing point on the window glass. For an inside mount, the valance can be shorter. If your window has mullions or defined panes, avoid having the lower edge of the valance fall just short of a horizontal bar. The result will be an unattractive, chopped-off look. If the valance is installed over floor-length curtains, it should be longer so that it is in proportion to the expanse of fabric underneath. In this scenario, a valance with tails could be a dramatic topper extending one-third of the way down the draperies at the sides of the window.

■ **Styles.** A valance can be pleated, gathered, shirred, or smooth. The fabric can match the rest of the window dressing, introduce a note of contrast, or repeat a fabric or color used elsewhere in the room. It can be hung on a decorative rod or a plain rod. The lower edge of the valance can be treated in a number of ways: it can be shaped, trimmed with a contrasting band, fringed, or adorned with a decorative edging, such as lace or braid. It can be longer at the sides than at the center. The upper edge can have looped cords, rosettes, bows, or tassels. You can repeat these details on other soft furnishings, too.

For durability and to ensure that they hang properly, many valances are lined. However, light and breezy styles, such as those made from lace, voile, or other semitransparent fabrics, are not lined. A lining can also be eliminated if the valance is made from a particularly crisp fabric such as chintz or taffeta.

When selecting a valance, choose a style that is compatible with your overall decor. For example, a gathered valance would look out of place in a contemporary setting, whereas a pleated or geometrically shaped one might be an excellent choice. Many pleated valances work well in formal settings, while balloon valances are frequently a good choice in a Victorian decor.

■ **Hardware.** The hardware for valances is as diversified as that for curtains. In some cases, the hardware and the style of the valance work together to create the overall effect. Decorative rods are a particularly good choice for tabbed valances. Clear rods are available for near-invisible hanging of lace and sheer valances. Double rods mean only one set of hardware for valance and draperies. Triple rods can accommodate an inner curtain, too. Some rods, such as wide continental rods and those with arched tops, actually create the shape of the valance. Install the valance rod so that the sides of the valance extend slightly beyond any underneath treatment.

smart tip

SIZING A VALANCE

To determine the most pleasing proportion for your valance before making any purchases, try the brown-paper template technique. Cut some grocery bags apart or purchase brown kraft paper. Draw a template equal to the right length and outline shape of your proposed valance. Cut out the template, and tape it in place across the top of your window. Analyze the proportions of the template. Is it too long? Too short? Make any necessary adjustments, and then note the final measurements.

OPPOSITE
The wide-striped fabric and decorative trim on the soft box-style valance and curtains add dimension and interest to the room.

RIGHT
A plain, softly padded cornice takes on a whimsical look with its appliquéd flowers, which repeat the colors in this child's bedroom.

balloon valances

A balloon valance gets its name from its full, puffed-out shape. Alone, it imparts a soft, feminine look to a window. The basic balloon valance looks like a shorter version of the balloon shade, but it is stationary. Used with floor-length draperies, the effect is more formal. When designed with side tails, it has a tailored appearance.

A puff valance is self-lined, opening at the ends so that the two layers can be pulled apart to form a pouf. The cloud valance is similar to the balloon valance but is fuller at the lower edge of the scallops. The shirred Austrian valance features scallops from top to bottom.

BELOW
This room is dressed up with a cloud valance, jabots, and a Roman shade.

Tailed Balloon Valance

Balloon Valance

Puff Valance

Cloud Valance

Austrian Valance

pleated valances

A pleated valance has a tailored, dressmaker look. Any common drapery headings can be applied to a pleated valance. The simplest version, the box-pleat valance, looks like a crisply pleated skirt. Other versions, such as the triple-pleat and butterfly-pleat valances, are pleated at the top and then released into soft folds. For the pleated-and-gathered valance, the area below the pleats is gathered up, forming a series of swag-and-jabot-like shapes. The cartridge-pleat valance consists of groupings of narrow, rounded pleats, spaced at intervals across the valance. On the bell-pleat valance, the unpressed pleats form soft cones of fabric.

RIGHT
Matching triple-pleat valances visually unite the French door and the window.

Box-Pleat Valance

Pleated and Gathered Valance

Cartridge-Pleat Valance

Triple-Pleat Valance

Butterfly-Pleat Valance

Bell-Pleat Valance

tabbed valances

With a tabbed valance, the drapery pole becomes an integral part of the window treatment. Because the tabs occur at intervals along the valance, this treatment is a wonderful way to showcase decorative rods and finials. (See Chapter 10, "Designer Hardware," page 158.) Tabs can be made from wide or narrow strips of fabric, ribbon, or cord that complement or contrast with the main fabric of the curtain. They can also be left plain or decorated with details such as buttons, bows, and rosettes.

Hardware hangers, such as drapery rings or café clips, can substitute for the tabs. A flat valance, one that is the same width as the window, is a banner valance. You can create a fuller effect by selecting a valance that is at least one and a half times wider than the window.

ABOVE
This pointed valance consists of sheer handkerchief-fabric panels, each finished with a glass bead that reflects natural light.

Tabbed Valance

Rosette Valance

Scalloped Valance

Arched Valance

Bow Tie Valance

gathered valances

The basic gathered valance is a long, flat valance with a rod pocket. When it is shirred up on the rod, the gathers form. Generally, the flat valance is two to three times the width of the window. When using large amounts of material, a light-weight fabric is better because it creates a fuller effect.

Specialized standard curtain rods, such as wide continental rods or arched rods, give the gathered valance a distinctive look. The Federal valance is created by pulling up the ruffle and securing it with a few stitches just below the rod pocket. Ruffled headers and shaped hemlines are another way to alter the look.

Federal Valance

Rod-Pocket Valance

Pointed Valance

Arch-Top Valance

BELOW
Used alone, a gathered valance in a bold green-and-white-check fabric dresses up the window while leaving the view unobstructed.

cornices

Although cornices and valances are often mistaken for each other, a cornice is a more permanent arrangement. In fact, some cornices are elaborate wood structures that look like architectural elements. Others are upholstered or otherwise covered with fabric to coordinate with the decor of the room.

■ **Materials.** Traditionally, cornices were wooden boxes that were painted or covered with fabric. Painted cornices often featured molding to heighten the architectural look of the treatments. Today, cornices are also made from buckram or cardboard attached to a cornice shelf or from a sturdy material such as foam core. Although these materials are stiff, they are easier to cut into curved and geometric shapes, expanding the variety of cornice designs.

The conventional box cornice has four sides: a face board (the front), two end boards (the sides), and a dust board (the top). The dust board helps deflect drafts—one reason why wood cornices were so popular in older homes.

Wooden box cornices can be painted or stained to match other woodwork in the room. They also provide a mounting place for indirect lighting, which can dramatically highlight the window treatment. Fabric coverings on wooden or foam-core box cornices can be padded, tufted, pleated, and outlined with piping for an expensive upholstered look. Cornice shelves can have fabric attached along the edges of the shelf, with or without face board and end boards.

■ **Scale.** A cornice should balance the treatment and be in scale with the window. Because of its architectural nature, a cornice is always mounted outside the window, usually with the dust board or shelf aligned with the top of the frame. The cornice should be tall enough to cover the window's upper frame, plus the hardware and headings of any treatments underneath. Generally, cornices are $12\frac{1}{2}$ to 15 inches long. If the window is too short or the ceiling is very high, install the cornice on the wall above the window.

Cornices can be custom-made or purchased ready-made in standard sizes. Cornice kits are also available for easy assembly from lightweight panels of polystyrene; you supply the batting and the fabric.

BELOW
Made of plywood covered in fabric, this decorative cornice is used to hide the hardware of the tailed balloon valance.

shaped cornices

Although a shaped cornice can be constructed from a cornice box, most use a cornice shelf. Buckram or cardboard—both easier than wood for cutting elaborately shaped designs—is attached to the shelf, serving as firm face- and end-board surfaces to be covered with fabric. The lower edge of a shaped cornice follows a geometric pattern. Scallops, inverted scallops, notches, and S-curves are common motifs. Piping or bands of trim can be used to emphasize the shape. A series of overlapping shapes, such as the triangles of the pendant cornice, can be individually reinforced and then attached to the cornice shelf. The cornice shelf can also support a wood crown that extends above the shelf; a fabric ruffle is attached below it.

BELOW

This brightly colored cornice has been cut to follow the pattern of its wallpaper border, enhancing the trompe l'oeil effect.

Notched Cornice

Shaped Cornice

Scalloped Cornice

Cutout Cornice

Geometric Cornice

Pendant Cornice

Wood Crown

Fabric-Insert Cornice

box cornices

A box cornice provides a solid base for a variety of coverings. In general, a box-based cornice has more visual weight than one with a shelf base. Stained or painted wood-box cornices are embellished with architectural details, such as crown moldings, picture moldings, and carvings. This style is particularly appropriate for large, formal rooms, and it is an effective cover for curtain rods, especially those that are high on a wall.

Upholstered box cornices are covered in mid- to heavy-weight fabrics. The fabric is applied over batting and can be pulled tautly and evenly to look smooth, or it can be manipulated into horizontal or vertical pleats. The upholstery can also be tufted with buttons or studs to give it interest. Sheer and lightweight fabrics are fine for hourglass, turban, smocked, swag, and other soft effects that are applied across the front of the cornice.

Pleated Cornice

Swagged Cornice

ABOVE
Covered in wallpaper, this cornice draws the eye up from the balloon shade and diminutive window seat.

Hourglass Cornice

Turban Cornice

Mock Roman Cornice

Wood Cornice

lambrequins

According to its traditional definition, a lambrequin is another name for a valance or a cornice. Today, however, it has come to mean a three-sided frame installed around the window—essentially a cornice with sides that extend down at least two-thirds of the window or to the floor. From a practical point of view, a lambrequin can conceal an unattractive window frame and help block excessive drafts. It also adds formality to the room. Because the long sides of a lambrequin are subject to bumping and banging, a wood base, securely anchored to the window frame or wall, is best. A lambrequin can be upholstered, painted, or stained just like a box cornice. Moldings and painted details often echo other architectural details in the room.

Arched Lambrequin

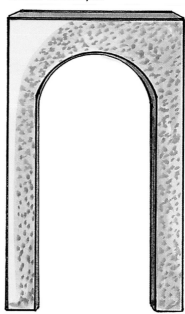

ABOVE
To make an exotic lambrequin shape, cut out the design from stiffened buckram; paint it to match the curtains; and then attach it to a cornice shelf.

Tapered Lambrequin

Shaped Lambrequin

design workbook
DRESSMAKER DETAILS

room to grow

The patterns on the box-pleated valances and curtains keep this room from looking too juvenile. (See also bottom right.)

warm and whimsical

The yellow-print piping and edge treatment on the valances picks up the sunny colors of the wallcovering and border. (See also bottom right.)

mix & match

An appealing combination of fabrics and patterns stay within varying shades of two analogous colors. (See also left and far left.)

materials matter

Eye-catching plaid fabrics are mixed in this window treatment, top left, which consists of a cloud valance, jabots, and a Roman shade. (See also far left.)

design workbook

ALL DRESSED UP

let in the light

A tailored window treatment with a crisp cascade valance in a neutral fabric ties in other aspects of the room and provides a contrast against the rich red walls of this library.

heighten the drama

To treat large floor-to-ceiling windows, use decorative valances and side panels that will draw the eye up and frame the view of the outdoors. (See also top left.)

simply a standout

Add a casual air to any traditional room with windows dressed in plain fabric and soft hues, left, or a simple scarf swag gracefully draped over a pole.

8

finesse with fabric

FABRIC BASICS MIXING PATTERNS
SELECTING A FABRIC DESIGN WORKBOOK

Fabric can evoke many different things. Brocades and tapestries look rich; velvets and wools feel warm; and lace and cottons appear light and airy. Good-quality curtains drape smoothly, pleat well, and have more body. Knowing how a particular fabric is made, the fiber content of its yarn, how the cloth was dyed, and whether it has been treated with a finish will help you to select the right one for your window treatment.

Did you know that a fabric's weight contributes to the overall effect of a treatment? Or that sheers allow light into a room, while opaque fabrics add warmth to it? Did you know that patterned fabrics affect the perceived proportions of a room? Before shopping, consider these facts. Then purchase fabric samples to see how they look in your home. This chapter will take you through the process, step by step.

Billowy translucent curtains made of cotton voile are highlighted with bright stripes of red ribbon.

fabric basics

Fabric consists of fibers that are natural—such as cotton or wool—or synthetic—such as rayon. When the fibers are spun (twisted), they become yarn. During the spinning process, natural and synthetic fibers can be blended, as in a cotton-polyester mix. Yarn quality depends on how tightly it is spun, how many strands of fiber are used, and the length of the fiber. To make fabric, yarns are woven on a loom. Yarns used lengthwise on the loom are called "warp;" yarns that run widthwise are called "weft." The same type of yarn can be made into a number of different weaves. For example, cotton can be woven into a damask. For a *plain weave,* the yarns are alternated over and under each other, from side to side, and from top to bottom. This is the most common type of weave. A variation on the plain weave is the *ribbed weave,* which features a thick yarn over a thinner one. A *basket weave* uses two pieces of yarn for each row in a plain-weave pattern. A *twill weave* results in a herringbone pattern. A *satin weave* has a shiny smooth surface. A *pile weave* produces loops that are then cut to create a soft surface; velvet

is a good example of this weave. A *Jacquard weave* requires a special loom that can do combinations of weaves, such as plain, twill, and satin.

A design can be woven into a fabric, becoming an integral part of it. Woven designs can be seen on the reverse side of the material. Some patterns are printed onto the surface of the cloth with dye, however. The color can seep through to the back of the material, but the design is blurred. Highly detailed printed fabrics can have as many as 20 or more colors.

The colorfastness of dyes varies, an important factor with regard to window treatments. Fabric colors will fade due to constant exposure to the sun. Darker and brighter colors tend to fade faster than lighter, neutral colors. For the best resistance to sun damage, natural fibers should be vat-dyed and synthetic fibers should be solution-dyed. *Ask about the coloring process.* There are special finishes that can be applied to fabrics to help resist fading. There are also finishes to repel stains, mildew, and wrinkles, as well as fabrics with a sheen finish, such as that of glazed cotton (chintz).

A fabric's *opacity* influences how it will look in a room. Even if the color is dark, a sheer fabric or one with an open weave, such as lightweight muslin, creates a soft effect and allows in light. Heavyweight fabrics, such as brocades and velvets, create a cozy feeling and keep out the sun, whether they are light or dark in color.

Be aware that there is a difference between decorator and garment fabrics. Decorator fabrics have a higher thread count and are more tightly woven, so they will hold up better. Most are 54 inches wide, whereas garment fabrics are 45 inches wide. The wider the fabric, the less yardage you'll need to make your window treatment. But decorator fabrics are more costly, and so you may not notice any savings.

Common Fabrics for Window Coverings

Textiles play an important part when it comes to delivering color, pattern, and texture to a window dressing. Here is a brief overview of some common fabrics used to fabricate curtains, draperies, and shades:

■ **Brocade.** Often a weighty fabric woven of silk, cotton, wool, or a combination. A raised, floral design in a Jacquard weave is a brocade's distinguishing feature. It is typically used for formal styles.

■ **Cambric.** A plain, tightly woven linen or cotton fabric with a sheen on one side. Curtain panels can be successfully made from cambric.

■ **Canvas.** A coarse woven-cotton material available in heavy or lighter gauges. Canvas is strong and inexpensive. It works well for shades.

■ **Chintz.** Cotton fabric, often in a floral or other all-over print, that is coated with a resin that gives it a sheen. Dry cleaning is necessary.

■ **Cotton Duck.** A cream-color cotton that comes in various weights. It is ideal for no-sew curtains. (See Canvas.)

■ **Crewel.** Plain woven, natural-cotton fabric with wool embroidery. Dry cleaning is required.

■ **Damask.** Another Jacquard material made of cotton, silk, wool, or a combination with a satin, raised design. This fabric is widely used for draperies.

■ **Gingham.** Plain-weave cotton fabric woven in block or checked prints. Its crisp look makes gingham popular for borders and curtain panels.

■ **Lace.** Cotton or cotton-polyester-blend material featuring an openwork design. Lace is favored for café curtains.

■ **Linen.** An unusually strong fabric made from processed flax. Linen is best when used in simple designs.

OPPOSITE
Red toile de jouy curtains give this small dining area an authentic, cozy French-country look.

LEFT
Dyed a vivid shade of red, these lined linen panels make a bold statement and complement the room's bright accent colors.

■ **Moiré.** This term actually refers to a finish, usually on silk or acetate, that resembles water marking. Washing removes the finish, so dry-clean the fabric. Depending on weight, moiré can be suitable for draperies.

■ **Muslin.** Ranging from coarse to fine, a plain-weave cotton fabric. Muslin is also called *voile.*

■ **Organdy.** Light cotton washed in acid for a crisp finish. Organdy is used for trimmings, borders, and curtains.

■ **Satin.** A silk, linen, or cotton weave with a glossy surface and dull back, sometimes with a moiré finish. Satin is not particularly durable but is fine for draperies.

■ **Silk.** A shiny fabric made from fibers produced by silkworms. Silk is favored for swags and formal draperies.

■ **Taffeta.** A silk-and-acetate weave that appears shiny and maintains shape. Taffeta is useful for borders and curtains.

■ **Tapestry.** A heavy, woven cloth that imitates handmade tapestries.

■ **Toile de Jouy.** An eighteenth-century-designed print of pastoral scenes on cotton or linen first produced in the French town of Jouy. Toile de Jouy is used for curtains, valances, or shades.

■ **Velvet.** Soft fabric made from cotton, viscose rayon, or polyester. Velvet features a smooth, iridescent-looking pile. Finer velvets are good for draperies.

mixing patterns

Mixing patterns can be intimidating, in part because it's subject to experimentation, judgment, and "eye." Responding to this fear, manufacturers provide an abundance of coordinated fabric collections, available through in-store design services. Such collections, selected by professionals, can save you a lot of legwork and still leave scope for your own input. If you prefer to mix your own patterns, try to match the scale of the pattern to that of the area over which it is to be used. The general rule is to use large prints on the largest parts of a window treatment, such as the curtain panel; medium prints on medium pieces, such as a cornice or a valance; and small prints on accent pieces, such as borders.

To experiment with mixing patterns, start simply. Geometric patterns often mix well together—stripes with checks, plaids, or dots. It is always easier to mix patterns that contain one or more common colors or have a similar level of intensity between the prints. A solid-color companion that pulls out a hue shared by two prints provides another connection. Exact matches are the backbone of manufacturers' coordinated collections. But to arrive at your own personal mix, you can interpret the principle loosely and experiment to see which pattern combinations work for you. Designers develop a knack for picking eye-catching combinations— and through experimentation you will, too. Look through magazines for ideas. Remember, however, that it is important to give your eyes a place to rest. Be sure to add a solid-color fabric or trimming into the mix, as well.

OPPOSITE
The application of contrasting weaves between the top portion and the hem of the silk taffeta curtains produces a radiant sheen (top left). A curtain's sheer white-on-white print provides a neutral background for a colorful corner (top right). The soft blending of melon, pink, and gold give a striped panel a vibrant effect (bottom).

ABOVE
Cotton-voile curtains in yellow and orange blend harmoniously into the warm color scheme of this comfy living room.

selecting a fabric

F inding the right fabric is a matter of trial and error. Your first choice may not drape as well as you wanted, or the color may be off by a shade. To help the process go more smoothly, follow these steps.

smart steps
plan ahead

Step 1 DEVELOP A COLOR SCHEME

Now is the time to pick a color for your window covering. You can establish it based on elements that already exist in the room—an upholstered sofa, a carpet, or even a favorite painting. Once you determine the main color for the treatment, choose an accent or two. Accent colors can be used for borders, trimmings, and even lining. (For more tips, see the section in Chapter 3 called "Color," on page 42.) Collect samples of various fabrics, and compare the colors until you find something that you like.

Step 2 CHOOSE THE RIGHT TYPE OF FABRIC FOR YOUR WINDOW TREATMENT

For the finished result to be successful, the fabric that you choose needs to suit the window treatment. Canvas is an excellent fabric for a shade, but it is too stiff to drape as a swag. A balloon shade needs a tightly woven material so that the scallops at the hem will hold their shapes and not sag. Don't judge a fabric by its looks alone; check the weight, weave, and dyeing process, and how the fabric should be cleaned. When you are using more than one type of fabric, make sure all of the materials are compatible in terms of weight and cleaning requirements. There are several things to think about before you decide.

BELOW LEFT
The toile de jouy pattern on the walls and window treatment coordinates with the blue-and-white furnishings in this cozy bedroom.

BELOW RIGHT
Tied back gracefully, crisp taffeta panels frame a pair of French doors, creating a glamorous theatrical effect.

OPPOSITE
A set of damask drapery panels features a woven design, incorporating a soft pattern into the room's neutral color scheme.

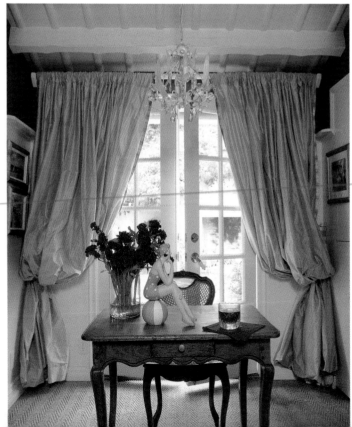

■ Durability. If you expect to have your window treatment for a long time, choosing a strong fabric is important. Some fabrics, such as silk, will fade or deteriorate easily due to sun damage. These types of materials require a lining or a special finish for protection.

■ Drapability. How the fabric should hang depends on the type of window treatment you want. Voile is often used for scarf swags because it is lightweight and hangs beautifully, but this sheer material may not have enough body for a pleated treatment. Thickly woven fabrics, such as tapestry, may be best suited to straight, not tieback, panels. In any case, fabric should drape gracefully into tight or loose folds.

■ Cleaning recommendations or requirements. This goes back to the issue of maintenance, as was discussed in Chapter 4, page 50. If you don't want to fuss with your window dressing, you need an easy-care fabric. If you don't mind investing time—and money—in the upkeep of your arrangement, you have more options.

■ Synthetic fabric treatments. A special finish adds to the durability of a fabric. It can provide resistance to sun damage, mildew, and stains. Some finishes give the fabric more body for better draping.

Step 3 CHECK HOW THE FABRIC LOOKS IN YOUR HOME

Once you've narrowed down the choices, collect fabric samples. Because a small swatch may not show a complete pattern repeat, try to get the largest sample that you can. You may be able to borrow a large swatch from the fabric store. If not, buy a yard to take home. Hang the swatches next to the window on which you're planning to use them. Take note of the fabric's opacity during the day and in the evening when the lights are on. How do the colors hold up? Colors that look good in the evening may appear washed out in daylight. As night falls, some dark colors can look muddy.

smart tip

A FABRIC'S DRAPE IQ

Test a fabric's draping ability by looking at a large piece in a fabric store. Gather at least 2 to 3 yards of material, holding one end in your hand. Check how it drapes. Does it fall into folds easily? Also look at the pattern when it is gathered. Does the design become lost in the folds? Ask a salesclerk or a friend to hold the fabric and look at it from a few feet away.

design workbook
SHEER ENERGY

dreamy draperies

Dressing windows with breezy opaque fabrics will soften the angles of a room, creating a casual effect. (See also left and bottom left.)

two-toned

Create a decorative element and add an air of distinction to plain panels by attaching a sheer color band along the bottom section of the curtains.

dressing up

Opaque curtains over shutters provide the backdrop for a vanity table, top left. The look is glamorous, fresh, and intimate at the same time.

fashion fabrics

Combining two lush materials in complementary colors, such as heavy red velvet over a light, neutral organdy, gives the window, left, the look and feel of elegance.

design workbook
PATTERN AND PERSONALITY

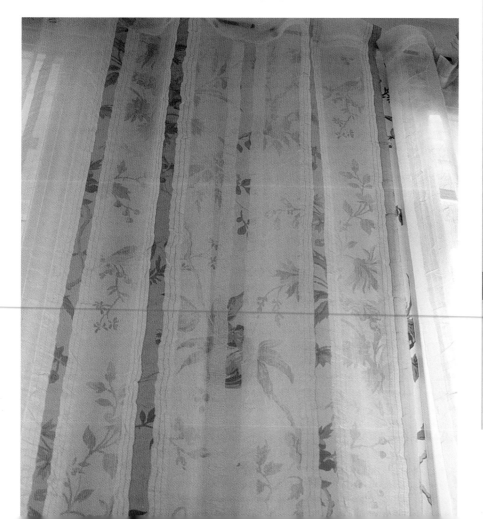

color impact

A combination of rich fabrics and vibrant colors can create a stimulating effect in any style room. (See also left and bottom left.)

have some fun

Add a whimsical look to a room by dressing the windows with a wide, bright striped fabric trimmed with a playful fringe.

a bit of nostalgia

Here's a new way to decorate with vintage cotton chenille. That once-popular bedspread fabric can be used as a curtain panel, top left.

subtle sophistication

Lightweight, gauzy panels with a green-and-orange stripe, left, are sheer enough to reveal the floral-print underneath.

9
tassels & trimmings

FINISHING TOUCHES THAT ADD FLAIR **TIEBACKS**
RUFFLES AND BORDERS **TASSELS** CHOUX AND ROSETTES
TRIMMINGS DESIGN WORKBOOK

Once the basic curtain design is established, you can truly make the arrangement your own. The decorative embellishments that you select reflect your personality, so create a design as unique as you.

Decorative embellishments come in many forms. *Passementerie*—French for tassels and trimmings—encompasses a whole range of traditional interlaced, braided, and fringed decorations.

Other accessories for curtains include tiebacks, borders, rosettes, and choux. Pleated, shaped, tied, or knotted, a tieback adds color and ornament to a treatment, as well as influencing its profile. Ruffled borders have always been consistently popular; appliquéd borders add a custom motif to a drapery design. Rosettes and choux, in all their many forms, punctuate swags, scarves, valances, and even tiebacks.

Applying decorative fringe in a matching color lends a finishing touch to this formal swag and tieback treatment.

finishing touches that add flair

No window treatment is truly complete without embellishments. These decorations accent notable features, create intriguing profiles, and inject extra color into any arrangement. How do you pick the right ornament for your window decor? Follow these easy steps.

smart steps
choosing details

Step 1 CHOOSE A COLOR

Tiebacks, ruffles, rosettes, and choux tend to be made from the same material as the curtain, but borders, tassels, and trimmings can complement or contrast the color of the face fabric. By choosing embellishments that subtly complement your window decor, you can enhance the entire effect. With patterned fabric, pull out a complementary hue from the design. With solid colors, try going one shade deeper for the embellish-

ment. Contrasting the fabric color can be trickier to get right, but the results can be eye-catching.

Take a sample of the curtain fabric with you when you shop for tassels and trimmings so that you will get the best color match or complement. Buy more than you need, not less. Should you come up short and need to purchase more, the dye from batch to batch will not match exactly. If you can't find the color that you want, some stores will custom-dye trimmings. However, many companies work with the trade (professionals) only, so you may have to purchase the embellishment through an interior designer.

Step 2 CHECK THE WORKMANSHIP ON TASSELS AND TRIMMINGS

Passementerie varies in quality—and in price. It can range from $2 to over $70 dollars for a tassel. Why is there such difference in price? It depends on whether the tassels and trimming are made by hand or machine. The type of thread used—such as silk, linen, viscose, or cotton—also influences the cost. All passementerie should be evenly dyed and consistently smooth in appearance. When buying high-quality tassels, look for hand-tied pieces without any glue. Trimmings should not have loose threads along the top and bottom edges or breaks in the lengths.

Step 3 THINK ABOUT SCALE AND PROPORTION

As was discussed on page 30 of Chapter 2, scale and proportion are integral elements in designing a window treatment. This is no less true when choosing decorative embellishments. A 4-inch-wide flat braid may overwhelm a café curtain, but a ½-inch border of ribbon may give it panache. Conversely, a rosette that is too

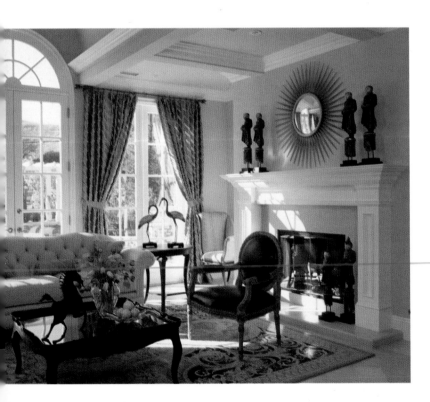

LEFT
This simple drapery treatment is enhanced with plain yet contrasting tiebacks, which also soften the hard edges of the French doors.

OPPOSITE
Silk balloon shades take on a rich, elegant look with the addition of a hand-sewn bead-and-tassel trim.

small will look insignificant on an elaborate pleated-and-gathered valance. Trimmings and borders can emphasize an element by giving it visual weight. Bullion fringe will call attention to the conical shape of a pipe tail so that it doesn't go unnoticed on the swag.

Step 4 REMEMBER—LESS IS MORE

It is easy to overdo decorative embellishments. The point of these accessories is to enhance the window treatment, not overshadow it. If you are designing a formal arrangement, you want the effect to be sumptu-

ous. Tasseled tiebacks on the panels and silk cording on the valance may look elegant; double-ruffles and tasseled tiebacks on the panels and rosettes, silk cording, and fan-edge fringe on the valance may be too busy, ruining the overall impression. If you prefer informal window dressings, keep embellishments to a minimum—one or two, at the most. For instance, if you are using prairie points on your shade, let that decoration stand alone. Add ornamentation slowly and sparingly. An economical way to test your choice is to make a quick sketch of the window treatment.

tiebacks

Most window treatments look best when gracefully draped. Tiebacks are strips of fabric that gently hold back a curtain panel, giving it form and establishing the final shape of the arrangement. They also provide the opportunity to show off a window dressing's contrast lining.

Traditionally, tiebacks were made from fabric, ribbons, or rope with tassels. (For more information about tasseled tiebacks, see page 149 in this chapter.) But tiebacks can be successfully fabricated from such imaginative materials as ribbon-covered hairclips, strings of beads, scarves, and belts.

Bow Tieback

Knotted Tieback

LEFT
Satin fabric draperies with a woven diagonal stripe are tied back and attached to the wall with a matching piece of fabric and covered buttons.

OPPOSITE
Corded rope is used as a tieback to emphasize the fullness of floor-length linen draperies framing a set of French doors.

Braided Tieback

Pleated Tieback

Ruffled Tieback

Crescent Tieback

To hang tiebacks, attach a small hook to the wall at the appropriate height. (Other options include using ornate holdbacks and concealed-tieback holders; see Chapter 10, "Designer Hardware," on page 158.) Sew metal rings or fabric loops onto the ends of the tieback, and then fasten them onto the hook.

■ **Fabric Tieback.** A fabric tieback is a narrow strip of curtain material that is lined. For a bow tieback, you literally tie a strip of fabric or a ribbon in a bow onto the curtain. Or you can use a loop of fabric with a pre-made bow attached. You can position the bow toward the front, side, or back of the panel. A knotted tieback is simply tied in the center, creating a decorative but unobtrusive accessory. A braided tieback consists of three strips of fabric that are plaited. It can also be made of welting (fabric-covered cording) for a fuller, puffier effect.

You can fashion a tieback from pencil pleats, too. Make sure to have a buckram backing so that the pleats hold their shape. You can also trim fabric tieback with a ruffle.

■ **Shaped Tieback.** Shaped tiebacks are formal, and sometimes considered dated. A template is used to establish the basic shape of the tieback. Some typical shapes are crescents, scallops, and rectangles with round corners. A shaped tieback is stiffened by a buckram backing. Although a shaped tieback is usually made to match the curtain fabric, it can be adorned with piping, rosettes, or buttons.

ruffles and borders

Ruffles and borders are attractive ways to finish off the edge of a curtain or the hem of a shade. Like other embellishments, these edgings add definition to a treatment's shape.

■ **Prairie Points.** Prairie Points are small squares of material placed at an angle to the edge of the curtain fabric, resulting in a zigzag border.

■ **Ruffles.** A ruffle is a border of gathered fabric attached to the edge of a curtain or shade. A double ruffle features two layers of frill. A pleated ruffle falls in neat folds.

■ **Borders.** A border can be as simple as an attractive ribbon, a braid, or a piece of contrasting fabric attached to the edge of a treatment. Appliquéd borders are cutout patterns sewn onto the edge of a curtain or shade. Some of the motifs include waves, leaves, Greek key patterns, and geometric designs.

ABOVE
This Victorian-style bath features curtains that complement the window's ornate ruffled shades.

Prairie Points

Ruffle

Pleated Ruffle

Double Ruffle

Appliquéd Border

tassels

The tassel is the purest form of decoration for decoration's sake. Consisting of a head and a skirt, a tassel is typically made of silk, cotton, linen, or wool. Other materials, such as jute or beading, are also used.

The tassel's head is constructed from a wooden form or bead covered with thread and tatting (a lace of looped and knotted thread). Flat, dome, ball, arrow, or rectangular forms can be used to shape the head. The skirt extends below the head and can be made of bullion fringe or cut or looped yarn.

A dangling tassel draws the eye to whatever feature it is accenting. It is often centered on a valance or a swag; it can also punctuate the notches of a cornice. A tassel can be a visual counterbalance to the long tail of an asymmetrical treatment. Or it can function as a shade pull. When you attach a tassel to a thick cord, it becomes a luxurious tieback.

■ **Key Tassel.** The traditional key tassel was originally used on key fobs.

■ **Rosette.** In this case, the rosette is a circular ornament of tatting, painted wood, or semi-precious stone baubles with a tassel attached.

■ **Frog Tassel.** Made of three loops of cording with a rosette in the center, the tassels hang from cording behind the rosette.

Beaded Tassel

BELOW
A tassel trim enhances floor-length draperies and matching valance.

Frog Tassel

choux and rosettes

Choux and rosettes usually adorn multilayered window dressings and swags, but they also embellish tiebacks. These decorations highlight any spot on which they are placed, so choose their location wisely.

■ **Choux.** A choux projects out farther than other finishing touches, so it is more noticeable. With a small piece of buckram as a backing, a circle of fabric is gathered and secured randomly, creating a ruched ball. For scarves, there is an easier and less formal way to make a choux: the fabric is knotted.

■ **Maltese Cross.** Made of curtain fabric or ribbon, a Maltese Cross consists of four loops and no tails. The center of the cross is disguised by a small circle of material or a fabric-covered button. This bow is a somewhat informal decoration.

■ **Fabric Rose.** Often made with wire ribbon, the material is gathered and secured from the center outward, creating a spiral of fabric.

■ **Ruffle Rosette.** This flower-like embellishment features a tightly gathered center with a ruffled edge.

■ **Knife-Pleated Rosette.** For the tailored effect of a knife-pleated rosette, the material is pleated and the ends are joined to make a circle. A fabric-covered disc is attached to the center of the rosette.

ABOVE RIGHT
Fabric rosettes are a noticeable way to decorate the ends of top treatments.

OPPOSITE
Fabric rosettes enhance the opulence of this period-style drapery.

Choux

Maltese Cross

Fabric Rose

Ruffle Rosette

Knife-Pleated Rosette

trimmings

Trimmings cover a variety of border-like edgings that are used to embellish curtains. This category encompasses gimps, braids, picot braids, piping, cording, jacquard borders, and fringes. Originally designed to cover seams and edges, these borders add definition to the shape of a treatment. For instance, the edge of a cascade jabot can be highlighted by fringe.

Trimmings are woven from fibers, such as wool, silk, cotton, or gold or silver threads. They can also be fabri- cated from other less-typical materials, such as chenille, organdy, or hemp. Fringes, in particular, can feature bead- ing, feathers, or stone baubles, which can sometimes glimmer as they capture a hint of sunlight or produce a soft chiming effect as they move in the breeze.

■ **Picot Braid.** The flat picot braid has a pattern of small loops or scallops pro- jecting from the side of the border.

■ **Gimp.** Gimp is a flat, ribbon-like braid of silk or cotton that is stiffened with a wire.

■ **Flat Braid.** Also known as a gal- loon, flat braid can be woven in any fiber. It ranges in size from 1½ to 3 inches wide.

■ **Cording.** Yarn is twisted together to make a cord. Thick cording is used for tiebacks with tassels.

■ **Jacquard Border.** A flat border woven on a Jacquard loom, Jacquard border can be 2½ to 6 inches wide.

■ **Fan-Edge Braid.** Fan braid has small looped cords in an undulating pattern.

■ **Piping.** Also called welting, pip- ing is a strip of fabric folded over a cord. Although it is available ready- made, it can be sewn by hand.

■ **Fringe.** With a skirt of twisted cords, fringe can be topped by a braid, lace, or crochet-work heading. The skirt can be ornamented by tas- sels, teardrops (fabric-covered balls), tufting (a cluster of threads), and beading. Brush fringe has a row of cut cords. Originally made of gold or silver thread, bullion fringe features thick, twisted cords. Campaign fringe has one or more rows of bell-shaped tassels; its name comes from the Italian word campana, meaning bell. Tasseled fringe ties together sections of the cord at even intervals. Looped fringe leaves the twisted cords uncut.

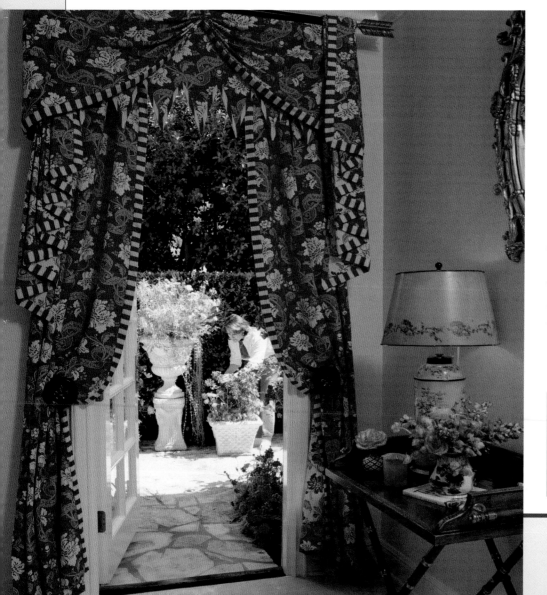

LEFT
Horizontal stripes add definition to a window treatment's edge.

OPPOSITE
Campaign fringe adds instant glamour to this swag valance.

Picot Braid

Flat Braid

Cording with Selvage

Jacquard Border

Fan-Edge Braid

Brush Fringe

Bullion Fringe

Campaign Fringe

Tasseled Fringe

Looped Fringe

design workbook
ADDING DETAILS

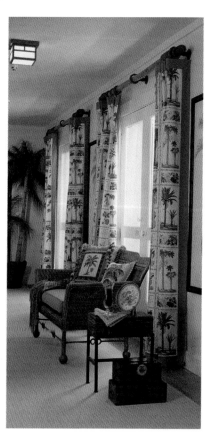

follow the line

Applying borders to a window treatment highlights the design while adding more pattern and dimension. (See also top and bottom left and right.)

a touch of class

This luxurious bath is subtle yet elegant with Roman shades trimmed in celadon green set against a pale damask wallcovering.

french country style

To create a focal point in this breakfast room, top left, a blue-plaid trim was applied to the window's valance, shade, and jabot.

framed in color

Simple floor-length printed panels are given a visual punch with the addition of a solid-color trim that frames each piece and coordinates with other accents in the room, left.

design workbook
FINISHING TOUCHES

completing the look

Decorative trimmings punctuate the overall style of a window treatment and can neaten unfinished edges. (See also top and bottom left.)

softly swaying

Applying fringe to the lower edge of valances and curtains will accentuate the vertical lines and provide a sense of movement to the treatment.

classic design

Rosettes and bows were used in the 18th century to decorate festoons and swags, serving as a focal point at the top. (See top left.)

main attraction

Trim can be used to draw the eye upward. Placed near the valance, a tassel-cord tieback adds to the fullness of the swag treatment and creates interest. (See far left.)

10

designer hardware

These days, window-treatment hardware extends far beyond the standard traverse rod or basic pole. Although some supports are intended to remain unseen, allowing the curtains to draw all the attention, other types are meant to be part of the spotlight. You can order custom designs, in materials and finishes to match your decor, but you can also find many fine choices in stores. Moreover, you can find style in all price ranges. Finials, holdbacks, drapery pins, and swag holders come in an endless array of motifs—from suns and fleurs-de-lis to curlicues and ram's heads. Even rods and poles have decorative possibilities. They are available in a variety of materials, including metals (brass, cast and wrought iron, steel, and gold- and nickel-plated metal), plastic, and wood. Faux finishes can customize a plain pole or rod, too.

Decorative hardware can introduce architectural interest in a room. Here it draws the chocolate-color accents together.

choosing hardware

Before you can choose your hardware, you have to evaluate your window and the window decor that you're planning to use. Will the treatment be installed inside or outside the window frame? Each situation calls for a different type of drapery hardware. An inside mount needs a rod or a pole that fits within the frame of the window. Suggestions include a basic traverse rod, a ceiling-mounted rod, a swivel rod, and a tension rod. There are no restrictions with an outside mount, so you can use any style of drapery hardware. However, when a window is poorly located, there are exceptions. A window that is too close to the ceiling requires ceiling-mounted hardware. Corner windows or a window close to a corner are other problem spots. Stay clear of using a pole that has large, ornate finials, because it will be too large for these situations. Instead, use an expandable traverse rod for curtains or swag holders for scarves because they require less space.

Is the treatment stationary? Or is it movable? Again, the hardware should suit the situation. For a stationary treatment, try a continental rod or a pole with finials. *Traverse rods* are the best for movable treatments. You can decide between a one-way or a two-way draw. A one-way draw pulls the curtain in one direction—either right or left. A two-way type draws the panels in opposite directions. The *headrail* anchors a shade or a blind, and it is the location for the track (if there is one). Vertical blinds can be drawn to one side or can split in the middle. The latter is known as a *split headrail* because, like a two-way traverse rod, each half of the treatment moves in a different direction. A *two-on-one headrail* features two cellular shades on one headrail, which is ideal for wide windows or sliding glass doors.

Will the hardware be seen? Or will it remain hidden? This also influences your choices. When the hardware will be on view, a pole with finials is the most decorative option. But if your design requires easy operation, a concealed-track rod may work for you. If the hardware will remain unseen, go with a traverse rod. It will allow you to move the curtain easily and can be tucked away under a valance or cornice.

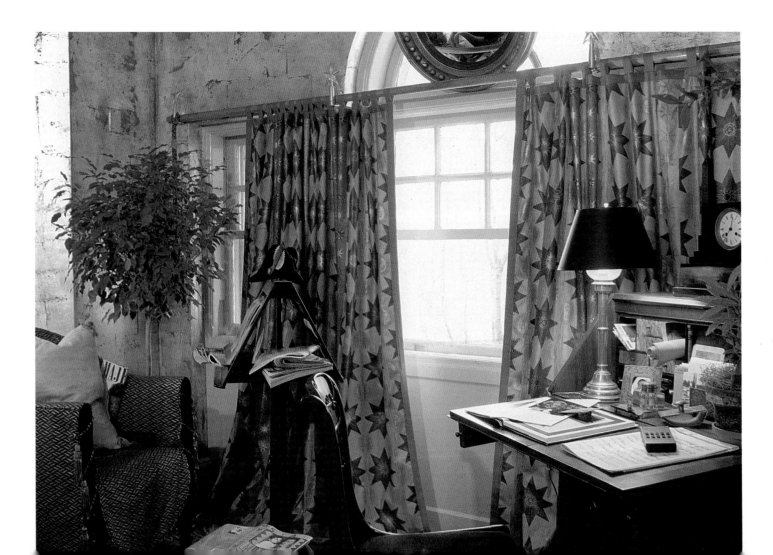

Operating Controls

There are different types of operating controls for window treatments. A *cording system* is the most common means of moving a treatment, but it varies with the style of the window decor. For instance, a cord pulley on a traverse rod draws curtains aside. For some shades, a system of rings and cords pulls the fabric up and down. In the case of vertical blinds, a chain system with a wheel mechanism moves the slats from side to side, as well as adjusts their angle. For any of these, you can choose on which side of the treatment to hang the cording system.

A wand is another way to draw window dressings, particularly vertical blinds. Basically, it's a plastic pole that hangs from one side of an arrangement, in place of the cording. When drawn by hand, the wand pushes the treatment along the track. When the wand for vertical blinds is twisted, it rotates the slats to any angle you desire.

Plan ahead where you want the operating controls to be located. In general, put an operating control on the side where you have the best access and where it is the least visible. If there is a cording system and a wand, keep both controls on the same side of the treatment. Operating controls for corner windows will look cluttered if you put them in the middle. Place the cording system or wands on the left for the left window and on the right for the right unit.

smart tip BRACKETS

Although it is rarely noticed, a bracket plays an important role in supporting rods and poles. If a treatment rubs against a window frame, an extension bracket solves the problem. It projects from the wall at an adjustable length, providing enough clearance. A hold-down bracket anchors a cellular shade or a blind to the bottom of a door, preventing the treatment from moving when the door is opened or closed.

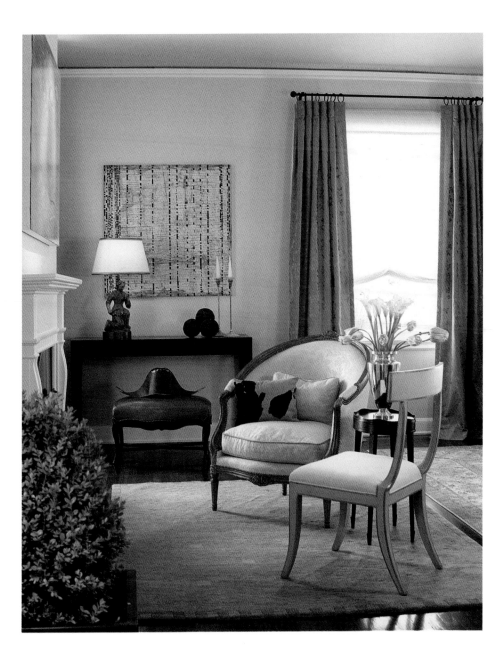

curtain rods

A curtain rod is the most functional means of supporting a window dressing. Because a curtain rod features a track system, it is the easiest type of drapery hardware to operate. The system consists of plastic or brass runners that glide along the track. Brackets are attached to the wall to hold the track (unless it is ceiling mounted). Usually, a cord pulley adjusts the runners, but some are moved by hand. If a rod is utilitarian and the curtain's heading doesn't have to be seen, the hardware can be installed out of view, typically behind a valance or cornice.

■ **Tension Rod.** A rubber-tipped rod with a spring mechanism that holds it in place within the window frame, a tension rod is useful for recessed windows. Lightweight curtains are the only option.

■ **Standard Traverse Rod.** There are two types of traverse rod: a basic track and an expandable version. A traverse rod is concealed when the curtains are closed. It is available with a one-way and two-way draw. This rod can be curved for an installation above a bow window.

■ **Ceiling-Mounted Rod.** Instead of requiring brackets, a ceiling rod screws directly into the ceiling or underneath the top of the window frame. It works well in a tight space, such as a dormer window.

■ **Continental Rod.** Stationary and $2\frac{1}{2}$ to $4\frac{1}{2}$ inches wide, a continental rod creates a deep heading on rod-pocket curtains, giving them visual interest. A continental rod is also used to make a rod sleeve more valance-like.

Expandable Traverse Rod

Ceiling-Mounted Rod

BELOW
The tension rod has a spring mechanism that holds it in place within the window frame.

Double-Track Rod

Track-and-Valance Rod

Swivel Rod

■ **Concealed-Track Rod.** A concealed-track rod is a hybrid between a rod and a pole. The front is a semicircular shape that looks like a pole; in back, there is a hidden track with a cording system.

■ **Double-Track Rod.** Two tracks, each track with its own cord pulley, lets you operate inner and outer curtain panels separately. A triple-track version, for two curtains and a valance, is also available.

■ **Track-and-Valance Rod.** If you want to hang a curtain and a valance on one fitting, a track-and-rod valance has a rail that projects in front of a traverse rod.

■ **Swivel Rod.** Handy where there is no stack-back space, a swivel rod is hinged so that it swings away from the window when opened. It works best on small windows, particularly recessed ones.

■ **Wire Rod.** A wire rod consists of metal wire threaded through small brackets. It can be easily used for bow, bay, and corner windows. Use a wire rod only for mid- to lightweight treatments.

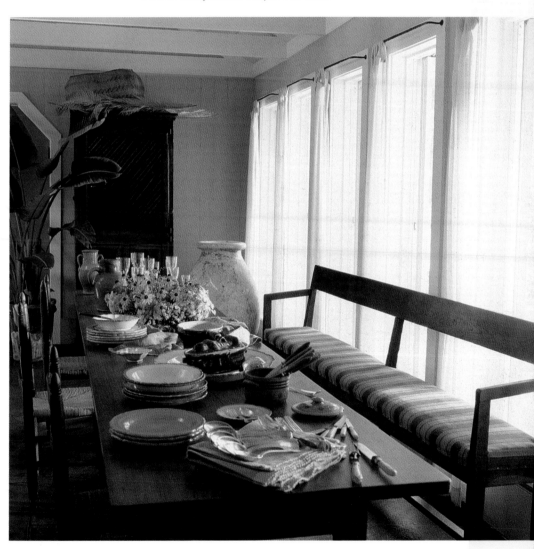

poles and finials

ecause of its decorative nature, a pole with finials can command as much attention as a window dressing. A pole is fixed to a window by brackets. (Use sockets for inside mounts.) Unless it's a tabbed or rod-pocket curtain, the treatment will require curtain rings or café clips to hang from the pole. These usually match the material and finish of the support. Café clips can be adorned with motifs such as stars or leaves.

■ **Wooden Poles.** The types of wood range from the inexpensive (pine and beech) to the expensive (mahogany and ebony). It can be left unfinished, stained, or painted. Finishes include metallic, verdigris, gilt, and faux marble. The pole can be turned to feature fluting (rounded grooves). To make rings glide smoothly, use silicone spray on the top of the pole.

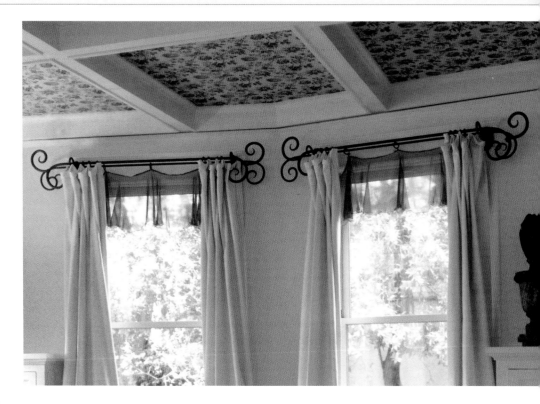

ABOVE
You can use small metal rings with clips to attach curtain panels to matching rods or poles as pictured here.

Ball Finial

Flame Finial

Shepherd's Crook Finial

Ram's Head Finial with Fluted Rod

■ **Metal Poles.** Brass, wrought iron, bronze, and pewter are some of the most-popular finishes. The diameter of the pole can range from narrow café style to wide cornice poles.

■ **Finials.** A decorative end to a pole, finials come in standard or custom-made motifs. They can be made of brass, copper, wrought iron, glass, ceramic, or wood. Some classic motifs for finials are scrolls, balls, shepherd's crooks, flames, ram's heads (and other animals), leaves, and arrowheads. For a creative touch, some finials can be turned into pegs for hanging tabbed curtains.

ABOVE
An elaborate pattern pairs best with a simple rod and finial that has enough personality to hold its own as an individual element in the window treatment.

Café Clips

Ceiling-Mounted Clips

Arrowhead Finial

Brass Rod with Crystal Finial

holdbacks

Holdbacks are multipurpose drapery hardware. Traditionally, a holdback is used in place of a fabric tieback. It is attached to the wall, near the edge of the window frame, and the curtain is caught behind it. For a sumptuous look, a tasseled tieback can be hooked on the holdback. When placed at the top of the window, a holdback can also function as a swag holder. Holdbacks can be made of metal, wood, or glass. Design motifs include rosettes, shells, flowers, curlicues, scrolls, and hearts. A concealed tieback holder is an adjustable plastic piece that holds the curtain away from the wall, preventing a tieback from creasing the fabric. It is not visible.

ABOVE
Holdbacks come in various sizes. Use one that is suitable for your window treatment. For heavy panels, you'll need a substantial holdback that screws into the window frame or wall.

Basic Holdbacks

C-Shaped Holdbacks

Seashell Holdbacks

Glass and Brass Holdbacks

Floral Holdbacks

Dogwood Holdbacks

other hardware

Drapery pins and swag holders are decorative accents for curtains. Drapery pins add detail to your window dressing. Used on lightweight curtains, the metal pins hold back a small amount of fabric. A swag holder is akin to a holdback, except with a looped piece of metal in which the swag is hung. Another type of swag holder is a resin corbel (a projecting bracket) with an opening for pulling through the fabric.

If you don't see the drapery hardware that you want or if you have your own idea, have a custom fitting made. You will need to work with an interior designer who has access to custom sources. Doing so is expensive, however.

Drapery Pins

Resin Swag Holder

RIGHT
Angled wrought-iron custom brackets accentuate the view and visually heighten the windows here.

Custom Bracket

design workbook

BIG IDEAS FOR HARDWARE

turn the corner

If you don't have an L-shaped rod, you can use separate rods and panels on corner windows. (See also left.)

the right ring

Paint or stain wooden rings, all photos at left, to match the pole, and make sure they are large enough to glide back and forth easily.

hang it high

You can install hardware on the window frame or directly into the wall above the window.

not too wide

Extend the rod beyond the window if there is room for the curtain to stack properly. Next to the mantel, left, the panel looks slightly crammed.

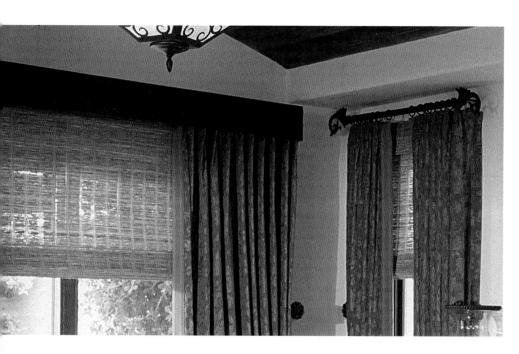

design workbook
TEXTURES AND SHAPES

decorative device

Elaborate, custom-made window treatments and hardware befits the formal decor of the room.

practical matters

A cornice conceals the hardware on the main window, top left. Holdbacks are used to keep the panels pulled back sometimes.

style matters

A bamboo pole and matching shade add an exotic touch to a design that includes pinch-pleated cotton panels, far left.

grand gesture

Metal rods that have been installed slightly below the ceiling allow the valances and curtains, left, to hang from high above the window frame for drama.

11

problem solving

EXAMINING YOUR WINDOW NEEDS   LARGE WINDOWS
SPECIAL SHAPES   GLAZED DOORS   DORMER WINDOWS
CORNER WINDOWS   DESIGN WORKBOOK

Even a beautiful window can be difficult to treat. In fact, the very shape, size, or location that makes a particular window pleasing may be the problem. A perfect example is any one of the variations on what are today commonly called "architectural" windows. Other windows can be equally frustrating. If a window is too tall, too short, too narrow, or too wide for the space, it can throw off all of the room's proportions. Other problems: how do you treat a small window that's tucked up high on a wall or extends all the way to the ceiling? What do you do with two windows that intersect in a corner, or ones that don't match at all?

Panels are perfect for these floor-to-ceiling windows; they can be easily opened to showcase the breathtaking view.

The solution lies within the the parameters of the window itself and the basic principles of good design. The rest of the decor, your lifestyle, and your budget will play a role, as well.

smart steps
creative thinking

Step 1 ASSESS THE PROBLEM

Is it the shape and size of the window that is causing the problem? Some windows are visually too short and wide for a room; others are too tall and narrow. Occasionally, mismatched windows end up side by side on the same wall or on adjacent walls. This is common in many older ranch-style houses where the bedrooms have standard-size windows and small, crank-operated awning windows. Some windows are poorly located because of architectural changes, such as when a room has been divided or a ceiling has been dropped. Is there a window that's too close to a wall? Or one that abuts the ceiling? Dressing large windows can also be difficult, particularly when you have two competing goals, namely privacy and light. Many of today's large homes have media and family rooms with a fireplace, a wall of windows, and no place to put the TV without contending with the glare. Unusual shapes can also be difficult. Cathedral windows, Palladians, arched units, ovals, triangles, glazed doors, skylights, and dormer windows all present challenges—ones that can be compounded by the size and shape of other windows in the room.

examining your window options

Sometimes windows are in locations that are difficult to treat. Or there may be one window that is out of place with respect to the size and style of the other windows in the room. There are many reasons why this can happen. Perhaps when the house was first built, its exterior appearance took precedence over interior consistency. Or the windows of a new addition don't match the old ones. Sometimes building codes have been updated, mandating a larger opening for a replacement window. Or an attic, originally intended for storage, has been transformed into an extra bedroom or a home office. What do you do with the dormer windows? There is a solution for each of these situations.

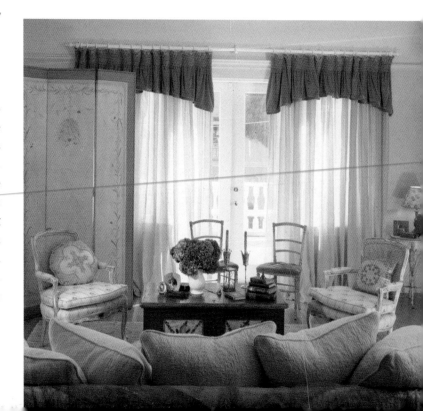

Step 2 IDENTIFY YOUR NEEDS

With your notes from Chapter 4, review what you need from the window treatments. Is there too much light in the room? Not enough? A window treatment in lively colors can help dispel the gloom in a room that is shaded from the sun by trees or other buildings.

Think about what you can see from the windows. Do you want to cover an unattractive view? Or is the view one of the reasons you moved there in the first place? Is privacy a priority? Daytime privacy? Nighttime privacy? Both? Think about how others see your windows. Large windows should be treated in a style that is compatible with the other windows on the same eleva-

tion. This is particularly important when the window is at the front of the house where passers-by have a curbside view.

Is the window accessible? Lack of access can make cleaning a problem with a very large window or a window in a hard-to-reach location. What is your budget? Even difficult windows have more than one solution. You want to find ones that are within your budget, in terms of initial expenditure and maintenance costs.

Step 3 LOOK FOR INSPIRATION

No matter what problem you encounter, there's a window treatment that provides the desired solution. In Chapters 5, 6, and 7 (pages 64–129), you became familiar with all the elements that comprise a total window treatment. The only limit to the number of ways these elements can be combined is your imagination. But sometimes imagination needs a bit of help. You can, of course, always call in the professionals, but even if you plan to do that, it helps if you have some idea of what direction you want to take. Study the photographs in this book; then flip through the pages of decorating magazines. Try to look beyond the curtains or shades to imagine the framework of the windows. Look for windows with the proportions, locations, or shapes that match the challenges you are facing.

OPPOSITE TOP
A coordinating element of matching curtains is used to balance the different-size windows and a set of French doors.

OPPOSITE BOTTOM
A pair of valances and sheer curtains frame a set of French doors, creating an illusion of two separate windows.

BELOW
Roll-up woven shades can control the amount of natural light or open up to provide a view of the sea and sky.

Poor Proportions

Proportion is a design consideration that is important to all the components of a room. When a window is too tall, too narrow, too wide, or too short, it throws off the room's entire design. Fortunately, window treatments are a creative way to camouflage any of these flaws without the expense and upheaval of replacing the offending window.

■ **Tall and Narrow.** Though tall windows are desirable in most cases, certain styles can run too high and appear too narrow, adding an unwanted element to your room's design. For windows that are too tall, use a cornice or a valance to visually lower the length of the opening. If your window is too narrow, extend the curtains past the window frame, covering some of the wall. With shades or blinds, choose an outside mount to make the window seem wider.

■ **Short and Wide.** Some rooms call for dramatic windows. For instance, a formal dining room may have a group of small sash windows that seem insignificant in the scheme. To visually enlarge them, run a valance or cornice above the top of the window, and extend the curtains past the window frame. For an individual window that looks too short, try the same trick—place the curtain rod high on the wall, and hang floor-length panels. Even

Mismatched Window Sizes

if you are using tabbed curtains rather than a formal arrangement, the two long curtain panels draw the eye upward, offsetting the short window. If the rod is visible, make sure the hardware is attractive and the finish ties in with the decor. Wide windows require different measures. To visually reduce the width, consider a floor-length curtain in a color that matches the walls to play down the horizontal form. Position the curtain so that it covers part of the window. Or consider a series of pleated or cascade shades to break up the horizontal line; the effect is increased if you adjust each shade to a different level.

Mismatched Windows

Mismatched windows in a room are windows unlike each other in size or shape and lack any distinctive features. The goal is to make them appear as similar as possible.

■ **Mismatched Size.** If the size difference is not too great, install a valance or cornice above all of the windows at the same height. This may mean mounting a heading on the wall above a window. Use an outside mount to disguise the position of the frames. Mount treatments under the header. Plan the larger window first, and then scale the treatment down for the smaller window.

■ **Mismatched Shape.** You can choose a different treatment for each window in this situation, but use the same fabrics. You can also link them by using the same hardware.

Difficult Locations

Sometimes a window is situated in such a way that there is little room above or to the sides of the frame, or the window may be out of reach. Despite the location, aesthetics, privacy, or light control may necessitate some coverage.

■ **Window Close to a Corner.** When one of two windows is too close to a corner, choose a treatment that doesn't have to stack back. Blinds with a swag offer a functional yet decorative approach. Other ideas include café curtains with simple valances or sill-length tab curtains mounted inside the window frame. For a single window, consider emphasizing the asymmetry with a curtain that is tied back to one side.

■ **Window Close to the Ceiling.** Because there isn't any wall space for the rod or track hardware, use ceiling hardware, or mount a lath onto the ceiling to support the rod or track and cover it with a cornice. If you choose ceiling hardware, the curtains will be stationary. Keep the style simple and the fabric lightweight. Or consider a cornice, which blocks the top of the window, helping to visually lower it.

■ **Skylights.** Most skylights are installed to increase light, so they are rarely covered. Sometimes, however, light is too glaring or makes the space too warm. A cellular shade with side-tracks to hold it flush against the window is a good solution. If the shade is easily reached, it can be moved by hand. Otherwise, a telescoping pole or electronic control is required.

A casual solution, which uses woven blinds, works best where there is a series of skylights. Mount the blind at the top of the skylight. Run cording down both sides of the skylight and through rings that have been attached to each end of the blind's hem. When lowered, the blind bows gently in the center, so leave enough above-head clearance.

Challenging Windows

Some windows present their own particular challenges because of their style or shape. The following pages explore solutions for many of these situations.

Window Close to Ceiling

Skylight with Cellular Shade

OPPOSITE
Mounting curtain rods above the frame makes short windows look taller.

BELOW
Matching valances allows two different-size windows to appear similar in scale.

large windows

Today, many homes feature a large window, such as a cathedral or geometric window, or several windows grouped together, such as a bay or Palladian-style window, dominating a wall. These windows are often an integral part of the architectural design of a room, providing access to beautiful views and allowing a maximum amount of light. In such cases, large or grouped windows are left untreated or framed with a swag. More often, however, the placement of these windows means that neighbors can see in and that the light can be overpowering during certain times of the day. To find the best treatment for these openings, consider the following ideas.

■ **Cathedral or Palladian-Style Windows.** A wall of windows is a common feature in a modern room, and one that can be daunting to treat. If lack of privacy is the problem, treat the lower half of a large window with curtains on a traverse or curtain rod and leave the transoms unadorned. Vertical blinds are another option, but they may look too severe for your decor. Try topping the

Cathedral Window with Curtain

Palladian-Style Window with Scarf

Angled Window with Shirred Curtain

blinds with a swag or a valance to soften the effect. Both of these arrangements show off the shape of a window while providing a covering when needed.

■ **Transoms.** Glare from the rising or setting sun can make a room uncomfortable. If harsh light comes through transoms, you can completely cover the window with drapery. Keep in mind that treating the window in this way may overwhelm the room and look too staged. Another option is to hang a scarf across the transom, which often blocks enough light to make the room comfortable again and is less obtrusive. You can also treat each transom individually. Try shirred curtains anchored at the top and bottom of the window by rods or vertical blinds and cellular shades in specialty shapes. A valance in a simple style, such as a chevron, can be hung on each transom. Remember, if the top half of a window is covered, usually the bottom half should also be treated to balance out the arrangement.

■ **Bay or Bow Windows.** When dealing with bay or bow windows, first decide how you want to treat them: individually or as a group. For individual treatments, try matching shades, blinds, or shutters, which look clean and modern. Or add tieback curtains for a soft style. A bow window needs a curved rod (which may require professional installation) or a wire hanging system. Instead of hanging curtains directly on the window frame, you can locate the rod on the wall above the bow or bay.

Bay Window with Curtains and Valances

Bay Window with Curtains Outside of Recess

OPPOSITE
Identical woven-wood shades create a bright and casual tropical look in a bay.

ABOVE
Leaving the clerestory windows uncovered allows them to figure in the architecture.

special shapes

Windows with special shapes, such as ovals, ellipses, triangles, and arches, usually exist because they add architectural interest, both inside and outside of the house. Sometimes the best solution is no treatment at all. If you like the look of a bare window but glare is a problem, investigate professionally applied window film. This transparent covering filters out the majority of the sun's damaging ultraviolet rays while minimally darkening the glass.

■ **Circles and Ovals.** For complete coverage, stationary cellular shades are available in custom shapes. When

Custom Shade on a Lancet Window

Shaped Cornice on a Lancet Window

Scarf on a Circular Window

Shutters on an Elliptical Window

Sunburst Curtain on a Half-Round Window

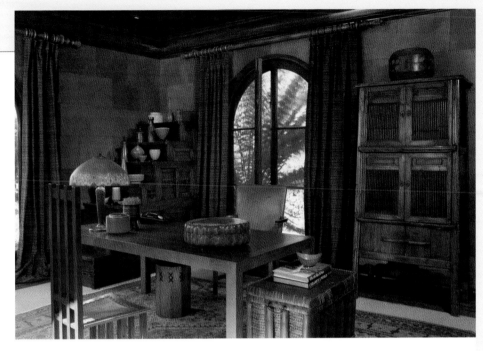

privacy isn't an issue, a scarf swag draped over a pole or through sconces is a pleasing choice because the curve of the scarf echoes the curve of the window.

■ **Half-rounds and Ellipses.** Half-round and elliptical windows can be covered by a sunburst curtain, which is a rod-pocket curtain shirred on an arched rod. The lower edge is gathered into a rosette. Consider custom shutters and cellular shades, too.

■ **Lancets.** These Gothic-style arched windows can be difficult to treat. Try a shaped cornice with flanking curtains or a specialty-shape cellular shade. A bottom-hung shade with a shaped hem is a custom item that provides maximum privacy. The shade is pulled up and attached by a tab to a peg or a hook.

■ **Triangular Windows.** Most triangular windows are left unadorned because they are usually placed above another window. However, strong sunlight can be a problem. Because of the angled shape, rod-pocket curtains are one of the few styles that work. Custom shutters, cellular shades, and vertical blinds are also attractive solutions. Remember that some of these treatments are stationary.

■ **Round-Top Windows.** You can either include or ignore the top. If you leave it untreated, you can hang any curtain, swag, valance, shade, or blind on the lower portion of the window. To cover the top, try a floor-length scarf that is gathered and secured around the curve. Or install a sunburst curtain or balloon shade.

OPPOSITE
The swag treatment follows the curve of the window's arch without interfering in the way the doors open.

ABOVE
Panels glide easily across the rod exposing the graceful features of the arched doorway.

Shutters on a Triangular Window

Scarf on a Round-Top Window

Balloon Shade on a Round-Top Window

glazed doors

No matter what type of glazed doors you have—French doors, sliding glass doors, or door-window combinations—the primary concern is leaving a clear passageway through the opening. If there is little wall space on either side of the opening, don't use a heavy fabric or a gathered curtain with a lot of fullness, because it is too bulky and blocks access. Instead, choose a medium- or light-weight fabric that stacks back tightly. If you are using a swag, check that it doesn't drape too low across the top where it can get caught in the door, particularly in the tracks of sliding glass doors.

Consider whether a door opens in or out. There are more design options for an outward-opening door because a curtain is less likely to block the door's operation. An inward-opening door with curtains can interfere with the movement of the door. Use treatments that can be secured above and below the glass on the door, such as some styles of shades, blinds, or shirred curtains on a pair of rods.

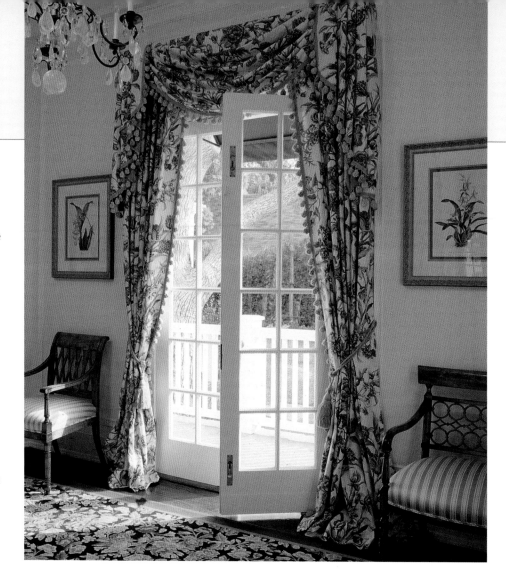

ABOVE
Make sure long curtains do not obstruct the operation of French doors.

OPPOSITE
Lightweight, sheer fabric that can be easily pulled aside softens this doorway.

Cuffed Curtains and Vertical Blinds on a Sliding Glass Door

Valance and Curtains on a Sliding Glass Door

**Curtains
on a French Door**

**Shades on a
Door-Window Combination**

**Blinds and Stagecoach
Valance on a French Door**

■ **Sliding Glass Doors.** Treatments that draw to one side, such as vertical blinds or curtains on a traverse rod, are the best options. Avoid any treatment that is mounted on the door itself because it will interfere with its operation.

■ **French Doors.** If the door opens out, a valance or cornice can be mounted at the top of the frame. If the door opens in and you want to install a top treatment, there has to be enough room on the wall above the door to accommodate it. A valance has to clear the top of the door. Otherwise, something that can be secured directly above and below the glass and curtains that stack back tightly work well. Shutters on tracks will require substantial stack-back space.

■ **Door-Window Combinations.** You can treat this situation as one large unit, using the same guidelines as for sliding glass doors. For example, a valance or a cornice can unify the door and windows. Or you can dress each section individually with a series of matching elements.

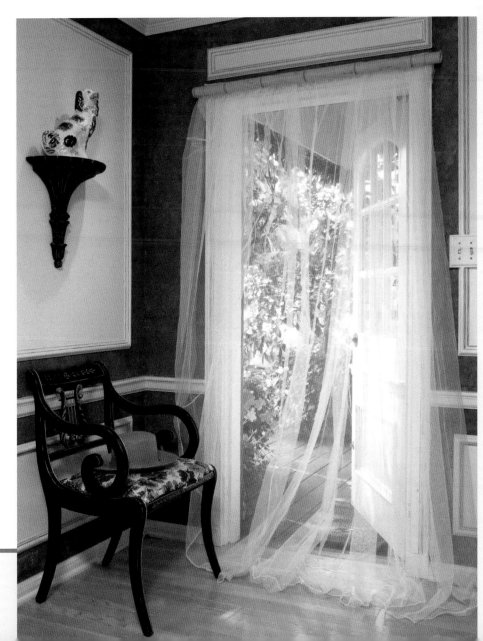

dormer windows

With dormer windows, you have the option of treating just the window itself or the area outside of the recess—or both. Swing-out poles work best for hanging curtains on dormer windows because, when light is needed, the poles swivel so that the curtain is against the wall. It's practical to use a lightweight fabric so that the hardware isn't overloaded. If there is enough clearance, consider a roller shade. For a dormer with a sloped ceiling, such as in an attic, there is a theatrical solution: hang a curtain rod on the wall outside of the recess, and secure the curtain with a second rod placed at the point where the ceiling and the wall meet.

Smocked Curtains with Two Rods

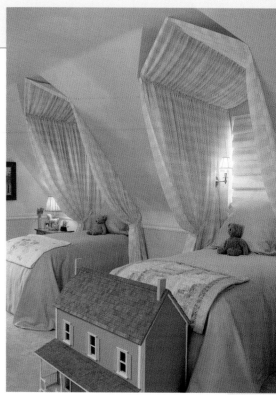

LEFT
A curved rod is custom-made to fit this bay window.

ABOVE
Attached at three points then tied back, this curtain treatment forms an almost-tent-like shape inside each dormer window.

Rod-Pocket Curtains on Swivel Rods

corner windows

When dressing corner windows, unify them with matching fabrics or a treatment that visually joins the two windows together. Pull them together with a valance or a cornice—both treatments turn corners neatly. Curtains are a good way to connect the windows, as well. There is also a variety of tieback options. The panels can be tied back-to-back, or they can mirror each other. Formal window dressings involve a combination of both styles. Try balloon or cloud shades, too. Have the shade extend past the window slightly so that the corner is visually filled in; the fullness of the treatment helps to cover any gaps. Swags and jabots also bridge the gap. Cascade tails, in particular, visually complement each other in a corner.

Balloon Shades

Curtains in "Mirror" Arrangement

**Swags and Jabots
with Tied-Back Curtains**

ABOVE
A corner rod and matching tieback curtains unify two different-size windows.

design workbook
A DREAMY BEDROOM

going together

Silk opera curtains look understated and elegant in this celadon and cream-color bedroom. (See also left.)

nice distraction

The left window abuts a wall, but the right window does not, so the designer pulled back the single panels to draw the eye to the mirror and painting on the wall between the two windows.

attractive opposites

The linen shades filter the light without darkening the small room. Together with the silk panels, there is a pleasing contrast of textures.

perfect harmony

An inverted-pleat header adds detail at the top, left. Curtain pins have been used to attach the panels to a hidden rod.

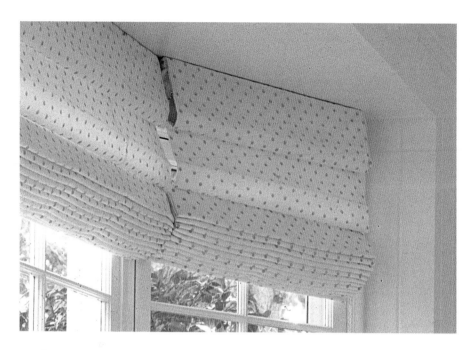

design workbook
WIDE-OPEN SPACES

keep It simple

Custom-made pleated shades are a practical way to visually connect windows and glass doors in various sizes. (See also left.)

repeat performance

Sticking with one fabric, in this case a pretty dotted print, for both the curtains and the shades provides another unifying element.

lights out

The blinds, top left, lined with a room-darkening material, can be lowered for privacy and light control.

neutral territory

The airy curtains soften the look of the window behind the bed while almost blending into the white paneled wall, left.

12

curtains you can make

Some of today's most fashionable looks for windows are relatively easy to make. Are you ready to try your hand? You could begin by making a pair of unlined curtain panels or a simple scarf valance. Gradually add decorative details to your repertoire, such as a knotted rosette or a curtain cuff.

If it's your first curtain project, choose according to your experience and sewing skills so you won't feel overwhelmed. Sheets are a great alternative to standard drapery fabric. Available in solid colors or in a variety of patterns, they are already seamed and hemmed for window treatments.

Splurge on your favorite designer sheets or shop the sales for the best buys. If you're not great with a needle and thread, experiment with no-sew treatments using items like iron-on seam tape and clip-on hooks.

Making a window treatment that's as perfectly tailored as these curtain panels may be easier than you think.

measuring windows

To make your project a success, take the complete measurements of each window for which you will be making a curtain. The illustration to the right shows the parts of a standard double-hung window. You can refer to it as you read the instructions that follow. These instructions apply to window treatments that will be installed either outside or inside the window opening.

For the most accuracy when you are measuring the windows: use a sturdy, retractable metal measuring tape; ask someone to assist you; and use a step ladder, if necessary, to get the higher measurements. Be sure to double-check your figures.

Inside Mount

For a window treatment that you will install inside the window opening, there are a few simple measurements to take: the length of the window from the top of the frame to the sill, and the inside width of the window.

Because some windows are not perfectly plumb, take these measurements in three spots, and then working with the narrowest measurement, round up to the nearest ⅛ inch. Do this for both the width and the length. Although this type of installation is more common for shades, blinds, or shutters, occasionally it is used for a curtain.

Outside Mount

Curtains, more often than shades, blinds, and shutters, are typically installed as an outside mount. Hardware such as rods, poles, and brackets are attached to the trim or wall outside the window opening. Decide where you want to install the curtain rod, and then measure the width from bracket to bracket. Add at least 3 inches to allow a center overlap. (If you are using a curved rod, add twice the number of inches the rod projects from the wall.)

Next, decide where you want the bottom of the curtain to fall: at the sill, the apron, or the floor; then measure down to that spot from the bottom of the rod, pole, or bracket. (If the curtain will hang from rings, measure from the base of the rings once they are installed on the rod or bracket.) Allow an extra 2 inches for the hardware.

basic panels

Making a basic, unlined curtain is an easy first project for someone with a modest amount of sewing skills. The materials that you'll need include fabric, fabric chalk or marker, coordinating thread, and shirring tape for a machine-stitched heading. You'll also need bent-handle shears, pins, needles, a yardstick (or a measuring tape), and a warm iron.

Trim off all selvages from fabric panels before you begin. The fabric for your curtain should measure two and a half to three times the desired finished width, plus 4 more inches for 1-inch-

making a mitered corner

FIGURE 1: Turn in the corner so that its diagonal fold intersects the point where the bottom and side finished-edge creases meet.

FIGURE 2: Turn under the corner, trimming it if necessary to reduce bulk. Turn up the bottom hem allowance twice.

FIGURE 3: Tuck in and smooth the edges of the mitered corner, and hand-sew it closed. Stitch the side and bottom hems in place.

wide double hems. Depending on the size of the fabric and your window, you may need more than one width (panel); you can use a partial width or even one on each side, if necessary.

Add double the desired width of the hem to the finished length of your curtain. (For example, add 2 inches for a 1-inch-wide hem.) If you're working with shirring tape, add twice the width of the shirring tape to the curtain's length.

First, mark and cut out the fabric. If there's more than one whole or partial width, lay them together, right sides facing; then join them using straight stitches. Don't forget to leave a 1/2-inch-wide seam allowance. Press the seams open. To clean-finish each seam allowance, place a row of zigzag stitches along each edge, or turn both seam allowances toward the seam line, and top-stitch through the folded edges.

For a well-tailored look, your curtain should have neat, even hems. Pressing is an important step, as is mitering the corners. To do this, lay the fabric right side down. On both the sides and bottom, fold over half the hem allowance and press it; then fold over the other half, pressing it again. *The folded hems must be perfectly even.* Unfold the hems. Turn in each corner diagonally, folding it at the point where the inside creases of the two hems intersect. (See Figure 1.) Press the corner crease, and then fold it under itself halfway so that the point is tucked in. To reduce bulk, you could trim away this excess instead. Press it. Turn up the bottom hem twice. (See Figure 2.) Insert a small fabric weight into the hem, if desired. Turn up the side hem twice.

Hand-sew (with a slip stitch) the mitered corner. Stitch both hems into place by machine or hand. (See Figure 3.) Press.

To finish the upper edge of the curtain, turn under the heading allowance once; then press. Turn under the heading allowance again. Press. Lay the heading tape a minimum of at least 1 inch down from the top edge; tuck it in at the sides, but leave the strings free. Pin the heading tape in place, and then machine-stitch it along the top and bottom edges. On one side of the heading, knot the strings, tuck them under the tape, and then stitch that side closed. Pull the loose strings at the other side of the heading until the curtain is the correct width, and then knot them. Check the width of the curtain against your window; untie the knots, if necessary, to make adjustments. Then knot again and machine-stitch the side closed.

smart tip PRESHRINK

Always wash fabrics in hot water to preshrink them before cutting and sewing your window treatment. This will also remove any glazing, which is a telltale sign that a fabric is brand new. The only exception is when you are using a fabric that must be dry-cleaned, such as a delicate silk or a fine velvet.

rod-pocket curtains

In order to make a row of gathers at the top of a rod-pocket curtain, the fabric should be two and a half times the finished curtain width. Add double the depth of the rod pocket to the length's measurement. (See "Basic Panels," page 192.) For example, if you want a 3-inch-deep pocket, add 6 inches to the length. Turn the top edge over twice, and stitch along the bottom fold. Insert the curtain rod into the pocket, and gather.

To measure for a rod-pocket curtain with a ruffle, add four times the depth of the rod pocket. That figure should be added to the length of the basic curtain panel. Turn the top edge over twice, as directed at right. This top allowance should be deeper to provide for the ruffle. Stitch into place along the bottom fold. Measure up from the bottom to the center of the heading, and stitch a second row across, creating two pockets. The top pocket becomes the ruffle; the bottom one holds the curtain rod.

BELOW

In this casually feminine room, floor-length pink-and-white-stripe curtains topped with a ruffle are a sweet touch. Ruffles are especially suited to stripes.

Making a Rod-Pocket Curtain

A Finished Rod-Pocket Curtain

Making a Rod Pocket with Ruffle

A Finished Rod Pocket with Ruffle

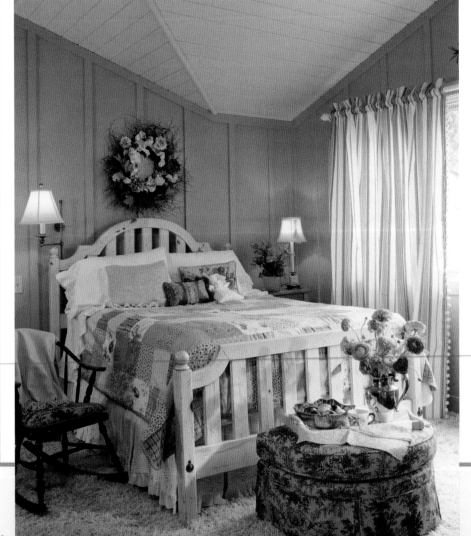

tabbed curtains

Tabbed curtains are a great way to show off eye-catching drapery hardware. Start with a basic curtain panel. (See page 192.) Tabs are typically spaced from 5 to 8 inches apart. Divide the width of the finished curtain by the space desired between tabs. Then add 1 to the number of tabs. For a 40-inch-wide curtain with 5 inches for tab spacing, divide 40 by 5, which equals 8. Add 1, for a total of nine tabs. For tab length, loop a measuring tape over the top of the curtain until you reach the desired length. To this length add twice the width of the curtain header plus two seam allowances. Double the desired width of the tab, and add $\frac{1}{2}$ inch for the seam—a 3-inch-wide tab needs $6\frac{1}{2}$ inches of material.

■ **Making the Tabs.** After cutting out the tabs, fold the fabric in half with the right sides facing, and stitch along the seam. Press the seam open, and turn the tab right side out. Fold the tab in half, with the seam line facing in; then turn in the raw edges, and pin the tab at the marking on

the top edge of the curtain. To secure the tab to the heading, stitch an X inside a rectangle. (See the illustration below, left.)

Other variations include bow ties and button tabs. To make a bow tie, fold a length of ribbon in half. Stitch that center point to the hem on the back of the curtain. For button tabs, follow the directions for regular tabs, as above.

ABOVE
A no-frills sheer curtain with a bow-tie heading creates simplicity in an elegantly decorated room.

Hand-sew one end closed, form a buttonhole in that end, and attach the other end of the tab to the curtain. Attach buttons on the curtain at the same intervals used for the tabs.

Making a Tab Curtain

Making a Bow-Tie Heading

Making a Button Tab

a simple scarf

Decide on the location of the holdbacks, and measure the distance between them. Measure how far down from the holdbacks you want the tails to fall. Add together the distance between the holdbacks plus twice the length of the tail. Add 1 inch for seam allowances. This is the cutting length of your fabric. The cutting width is the width of your fabric panel after trimming the selvages.

Based on the measurements, cut a rectangle of fabric. Fold each end in to meet at the center of the fabric; crease each fold. Unfold; mark a diagonal line from each upper corner down to the crease at the lower edge. Cut along these lines, and use this as a pattern for cutting out the lining. Right sides facing, sew fabrics together, leaving a small opening. Turn the fabrics right side out. Slip-stitch the opening closed; press. Fold the scarf into accordion pleats, and drape it over the holdbacks.

ABOVE
A softly draping swag appears to be one long piece of fabric but is actually made up of several separate elements.

Making a Simple Scarf

STEP 1. Cut out the fabric.

STEP 2. Make accordion pleats.

STEP 3. Install the finished scarf in the holdbacks.

decorative details

Here are two quick projects. The first is an easy rosette detail that you can make from a short length of fabric and add to a simple scarf. The second is a cuff, used to create an attractive layered effect on tab and bow-tie curtains.

■ **Easy Rosette:** Knot a length of fabric on top of your wrist, and leave the ends hanging. (See Step 1.) Then tie the two ends together below your wrist, and tighten. (See Step 2.) Last, slip the material off your hand, and tighten the rosette a bit more. But don't overdo it. Leave some fullness in the rosette. (See Step 3.) Do this for each rosette. Lightweight materials, such as lace and voiles, work best for this detail.

ABOVE
Handmade rosettes are a simple way to enhance an elegant swag.

**Making a
Knotted Rosette**

STEP 1. Knot the fabric loosely.

STEP 2. Tie the ends together.

STEP 3. Fluff the rosette.

Making a Curtain Cuff

■ **Charming Cuff:** The measurement for the cuff is double its depth plus ½ inch for the fold. Add this total to the length of the basic curtain panel. (See page 192.)

At the top of the curtain, make a ½-inch fold, and secure. Fold the fabric down double the distance of the cuff. Then fold up half of the material. Baste the top edge of the cuff into place. Slip-stitch or machine-stitch the cuff in place; remove basting. Add tabs or bow ties. (See page 195.)

STEP 1. Fold the fabric.

STEP 2. Stitch the cuff.

LEFT
Gauzy fabric embellished with cuffs creates a romantic effect.

design workbook
WISTFUL AND ROMANTIC

easy does it

This window treatment looks elaborate but was simple to create. Hand-made rosettes draw the eye up to the cherub plaques, left.

all puffed up

Gracefully draped opaque fabric is puffed and tied between windows to create the look of one continuous treatment. (See also above left.)

suncatcher

Although this window treatment is substantial, left, its gauzy white fabric allows sunlight to filter into the room, keeping it bright and airy.

one for all

Using the same fabric for both the swags and the bishop's sleeve vertical panels maintains the romantic feel of the room. (See also left.)

design workbook
BRIGHT AND CHEERFUL

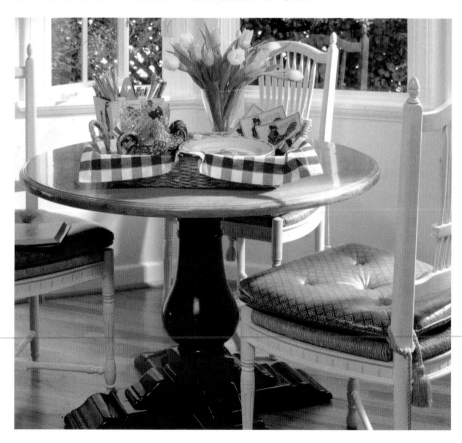

cover-up

A simple rod-pocket valance is an attractive and cost-effective way to soften the look of practical shades or blinds. Here, they add color and pattern.

a little something

A bold red trim echoes other colorful accents. Trim is easy to add with a needle and thread or a no-sew alternative. (See also above left.)

wide open

In a sunny spot flanked by windows, left, the best treatment is one that is there when you need it and tucked away when you don't.

make it your own

The print on the valances in these photos ties in with the room's French-country theme. Choose your colors and fabrics to establish your personal style.

appendix

Templates are an easy way to see different styles on a particular widow.
Simply photocopy, enlarge, or color them too try out different looks.
Mix and match until you find an arrangement that you like.

Double-Hung And Casement-Window Templates

Double-hung Window

Casement Window

Double-hung Window

Casement Window

Tab Valance

Cornice

Double-Hung And Casement-Window Templates

Tapered Valance

Triple Swag

Triple Swag

Double Swag

Single Swag

Single Swag

Roman Shade

Balloon Shade

Asymmetrical Scarf

Curtain Rod

Balloon Valance

Double-Hung And Casement-Window Templates

Shutters

Scarf

Blinds

Vertical Blinds

Plantation Shutters

Tab Café Curtains

Rod-Pocket Curtains

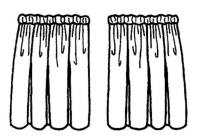

Café Curtains

Picture-Window Templates

Picture Window

Tab Valance

Tab Café Curtains

Vertical Blinds

Balloon Shade

Balloon Valance

Café Curtains

Picture-Window Templates

Rod-Pocket Curtains

Café Shutters

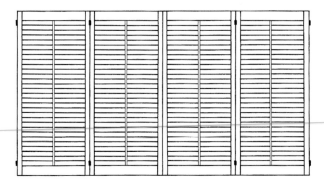

Plantation Shutters

Bow-Window Templates

Bow Window

Balloon Valance

Tab Valance

Plantation Shutters

Bow-Window Templates

Rod-Pocket Curtains

Tab Café Curtains

Bay-Window Templates

Bay Window

Bay-Window Templates

Rod-Pocket Curtains

Balloon Valance

Tab Café Curtains

Bay-Window Templates

Plantation Shutters

Tab Valance

Rod-Pocket Curtains with Tiebacks

Bay-Window Templates

Blinds

Vertical Blinds

Café Shutters

Large- and Small-Arch Templates

Large Arch

Large Shutter

Scarf

Small Arch

Small Shutter

Sunburst Curtain

Sliding-Glass-Door and French-Door Templates

Sliding Glass Door

French Door

Vertical Blinds

Blinds (French Door Only)

Sliding-Glass Door, French-Door, and Cathedral-Door Templates Cont'd

Floor-Length Scarf with Rosettes

Rod-Pocket Curtains

Triple-Pleat Curtains

Tab Curtain

Cathedral-Door Templates

Cathedral Door (left)   **Cathedral Door (right)**

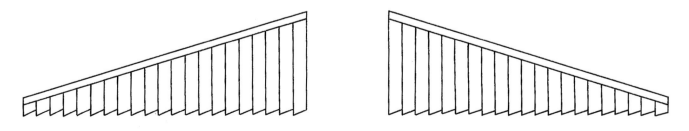

Vertical Blinds (Cathedral Doors Only)

resource guide

The following list of manufacturers and associations is meant to be a general guide to additional industry and product-related sources. It is not intended as a listing of products and manufacturers represented by the photographs in this book.

American Society of Interior Designers, Inc. (ASID)
202-546-3480
www.asid.org
Provides consumers with information about interior-design subjects, including design programs and continuing education. Its Web site offers a designer referral service.

Atlas Homewares
800-799-6755
www.atlashomewares.com
Sells decorative hardware. Ideas for unique tiebacks are found on the Web site.

Brewster Wallcovering Co.
800-958-9580
www.brewp.com
Manufactures valances, borders, fabric, and wallpaper in a wide variety of styles and collections.

Calico Corners
800-213-6366
www.calicocorners.com
Sells decorator fabric. In-store services include design consultation and custom window-treatment fabrication.

Comfortex Window Fashions
800-843-4151
www.comfortex.com
Manufacturers custom window treatments. The product line includes sheer and pleated shades, wood shutters, and blinds.

Country Curtains
800-456-0321
www.countrycurtains.com
Sells ready-made curtains, shades, blinds, hardware, and accessories, in-store and on-line.

Eisenhart Wallcoverings Company
800-931-9255
www.eisenhartwallcoverings.com
Manufactures coordinated wallcoverings and fabrics.

F. Schumacher & Co.
212-415-3900
www.fschumacher.com
Manufactures coordinated wallcoverings and fabrics.

Graber Window Fashions
Spring Industries
800-221-6352
www.springs.com
Manufactures shades, blinds, and window hardware.

Hancock Fabrics
877-322-7427
www.hancockfabrics.com
Sells fabric and trimmings.

Hunter Douglas, Inc.
800-789-0331
www.hunterdouglas.com
Manufactures shades, blinds, and shutters. Its Web site directs consumers to designers, dealers, and installers.

Kirsch Window Fashions
800-538-6567
www.kirsch.com
Manufactures blinds, rods, shades, and holdbacks.

Levolor
800-538-6567
www.levolor.com
Manufactures a variety of blinds, including vertical, wood, and cordless types, as well as cellular shades.

Motif Designs
800-431-2424
www.motif-designs.com
Manufactures a coordinated line of fabrics and wallcoverings.

Plow and Hearth
800-494-7544
www.plowhearth.com
Catalog company that sells insulated curtains, hardware, valances, and sheers.

Portsmouth Drapery Hardware Co.
603-433-4610
www.draperyhardware.com
Manufactures fabrics and easy-to-install window hardware for residential and commercial use.

Scalamandré
800-932-4361
www.scalamandre.com
Manufactures and imports high-end fabrics and trimmings for the professional interior-design trade.

Seabrook Wallcoverings
901-320-3500
www.seabrookwallcoverings.com
Manufactures and distributes coordinated wallcoverings and fabrics.

Smith & Noble
800-560-0027
www.smithandnoble.com
Catalog source for ready-made and semi-custom window treatments, fabric, and hardware.

Spiegel
800-474-5555
www.spiegel.com
Catalog source for window treatments, hardware, and related embellishments.

Springs Industries, Inc.
888-926-7888
www.springs.com
Manufactures window treatments, including blinds and shutters.

Thibaut Wallcoverings
973-643-3777
www.thibautdesign.com
Manufactures coordinated wallcoverings and fabrics.

Waverly
800-423-5881
www.waverly.com
Manufacturers coordinated wallcoverings and fabrics, as well as ready-made curtains and accessories.

Window Coverings of America Association (WCAA)
888-298-9222
www.wcaa.org
A nonprofit trade organization that represents the window-coverings industry.

York Wallcoverings
717-846-4456
www.yorkwall.com
Manufactures coordinated fabrics, wallpaper, and borders.

glossary OF WINDOW TREATMENT TERMS

Austrian Shade: A fabric shade that falls in cascading scallops and is operated with a cord.

Awning Window: A hinged, horizontal window that opens outward and is often operated with a crank system.

Balloon Shade: A fabric shade that falls in full blousy folds at the bottom and is operated with a cord.

Bay Window: A multiple-window unit projecting out from the exterior wall of a house, forming an angled recess inside the house.

Bow Window: A large window that is similar to a bay unit, but the recess is curved.

Box Pleats: Two folds turned toward each other, creating a flat-fronted pleat.

Brackets: Hardware attached to the window to support the curtain rod or pole.

Brocade: A weighty, typically formal fabric in silk, cotton, or wool. It is distinguished by a raised, often floral, design in a jacquard weave.

Buckram: A coarse fabric, stiffened with glue, that is used to give body and shape to curtain headings.

Cased Heading: Fabric folded over and anchored with a row of stitches to form a rod pocket.

Casement Window: A hinged vertical window that opens in or out and is often operated with a crank mechanism.

Chintz: A cotton fabric that is coated with a resin to give it a sheen.

Clerestory Window: A window set near the ceiling.

Cloud Shade: A balloon shade that has a gathered or pleated heading and is operated with a cord.

Cornice: A projecting, decorative box that is installed above a window.

Damask: A jacquard-weave fabric made of cotton, silk, wool, or a combination with a satin, raised design. Widely used for draperies.

Dormer Window: A window set into the front face of a dormer.

Double-Hung Window: The most common type, consisting of two sash, one atop the other, which slide up and down to open and close the window.

Draping: A technique of folding, looping, and securing fabric in graceful folds and curves. The drape of a curtain is the way it hangs.

Face Fabric: The primary, outer fabric used in a window treatment.

Finial: The decorative ends of a curtain rod or pole.

Flemish Heading: A pleat that is stuffed with batting for a puffed appearance; also called a "Goblet Pleat."

Festoon Shade: A shade that is made of gathered fabric, such as an Austrian, balloon, or cloud shade.

French Door: A door, typically with 12 divided panes of glass, used alone or in pairs. It is also used as a fixed window.

Goblet Pleat: See *Flemish Heading.*

Heading: The horizontal area at the top of a curtain. Its style determines how a curtain hangs.

Holdback: Curtain hardware made of metal, wood, or glass. It is installed into the wall or on the window trim and is used in place of a tieback.

Interlining: Made of lightweight, opaque fabric, a layer between the curtain fabric and the lining that adds body and blocks light.

Jabot: The vertical element that hangs at the side of a sweeping scallop (swag) or crescent-shape drape of fabric at the top of a window.

Jacquard: A loom, named after its inventor, that uses punched cards to weave intricate raised designs. Brocade and damask are jacquard fabrics.

Lambrequin: A painted board or stiffened fabric that surrounds the top and side of a window or a door. Historically, it also was drapery that hung from a shelf, such as a mantel.

Lining: An underlayer of fabric that is added to a curtain for extra body and to filter light and air.

Miter: A sewing technique for creating a flat corner where two hemmed edges of fabric meet.

Moiré: A fabric finish on silk or acetate, intended to resemble water marking.

Muslin: A plain-weave cotton; also called "voile."

Pattern Matching: To align a repeating pattern when joining together two pieces of fabric.

Piping: An edging made of cording encased in bias-cut fabric.

Pleater Hooks: Metal hooks that are inserted into pleating tape to create pleats in a curtain heading.

Pleating Tape: A cotton or nylon strip, with drawstrings, that is sewn onto the back of the heading to make pleats.

Roller Shade: A fabric or vinyl shade that is attached to a spring-loaded roller.

Roman Shade: A fabric shade that falls into flat, horizontal folds. It is raised by a cord system.

Stack-Back: The space along the sides of a window taken up by a curtain when it is drawn back.

Swag: A sweeping scallop or crescent-shape drape of fabric at the top of a window. In a swag-and-jabot treatment, it is the center element that is flanked by one or a set of tails (jabots).

Taffeta: A silk-and-acetate weave that appears shiny and maintains shape. It is used for formal-style curtains, draperies, and shades.

Tail: See *Jabot.*

Tieback: A fabric strip or cord used to hold curtains open; also a style of curtain.

Toile de Jouy: An eighteenth-century design of pastoral, allegorical, or romantic scenes printed in one color on cotton or linen. It is named for the French town, Jouy, where it orginated. Today, toile is reproduced in numerous colors and on various fabrics.

Traverse Rod: A rod from which curtains are hung that features a track system or runners.

Valance: A short length of fabric that hangs along the top of a window, with or without a curtain underneath.

Voile: See *Muslin.*

index

photo credits

page 5: Nancy Hill page 6: davidduncanlivingston.com page 8–9: davidduncanlivingston.com page 10: *left* davidduncanlivingston.com; *right* Tria Giovan page 12 Mark Samu, design: Eileen Boyd Interiors page 14: Karyn R. Millet, Bonesteel Trout Hall page 15: Mark Samu, design: Eileen Boyd Interiors page 16: Bob Greenspan page 17: Anne Gummerson page 18: Mark Lohman page 19: Mark Lohman pages 20–21: Mark Samu page 22: *top* Olson Photography, LLC; *bottom* Mark Samu page 23: Bjorg Magnea page 24: davidduncanlivingston.com pages 26-29: davidduncanlivingston.com page30: Jessie Walker page 31: davidduncanlivingston.com page 32-33: Eric Roth page 34: *top* melabee m miller, design: Christine Thompson; *bottom* Eric Roth page 35: Eric Roth page 36: davidduncanlivingston.com page 37: melabee m miller, design Jennifer Pacca page 38: davidduncanlivingston.com page 40: Roy Inman page 41: davidduncanlivingston.com page42: *top* Tony Giammarino/ Giammarino & Dworkin; *bottom* Mark Lohman page 43: Mark

Lohman page 44: davidduncanlivingston.com page 45: Eric Roth, design: Susan Sargent designs page 46–47: Mark Samu pages 48–49: *all* melabee m miller, design: Nancee Brown page 50: Mark Samu page 52: *top* davidduncanlivingston.com, *bottom* Mark Lohman page 53: davidduncanlivingston.com page 54: melabee m miller, design: Jennifer Pacca page 55: Bob Greenspan, stylist: Susan Andrews page 56: Jessie Walker page 57: davidduncanlivingston.com page 58: Eric Roth, design: Susan Sargent Warner page 59: Eric Roth pages 60–61: *all* Karyn R. Millet pages 62–63: *all* Eric Roth page 64: Mark Lohman page 66: Jessie Walker pages 67–68: davidduncanlivingston.com pages 69, 72: Mark Lohman page 73: *all* davidduncanlivingston.com page 74: Mark Lohman page 75: davidduncanlivingston.com page 77: Jessie Walker page 79–80: davidduncanlivingston.com pages 81–86: *all* Mark Lohman page 88: davidduncanlivingston.com page 89: *all* davidduncanlivingston.com page 91: davidduncanlivingston.com page 92: Tony

Giammarino/Giammarino & Dworkin page 93: davidduncanlivingston.com page 94: Mark Lohman page 95: davidduncanlivingston.com page 96: melabee m miller, designer: Anne Goldsmith pages 97–99: davidduncanlivingston.com pages 100–101: Mark Lohman page 102: Tony Giammarino/Giammarino & Dworkin page 103: Mark Lohman page 104: *all* davidduncanlivingston.com page 105: Mark Lohman page 106: *top* davidduncanlivingston.com, *bottom* Mark Lohman page 107: Tria Giovan pages 108–114: Mark Lohman pages 115–116: davidduncanlivingston.com pages 117–118: Mark Lohman page 119: Tony Giammarino/Giammarino & Dworkin page 120: Eric Roth page 121: Jessie Walker page 122: Mark Lohman page 123: Eric Roth page 124: Phillip H. Ennis Photography, design: Gail Green page 125: Stickley Photo-Graphic pages 126–127: Mark Lohman page 128: *top* davidduncanlivingston.com, *bottom* Jessie Walker page 129: davidduncanlivingston.com page 130: Eric Roth page 132: Mark Lohman pages 133–135: Eric Roth page 136: *left*

Mark Lohman; *right* Eric Roth page 137: Mark Lohman pages 138–141: Eric Roth pages 142–148: Mark Lohman page 149: davidduncanlivingston.com pages 150-156: Mark Lohman page 158: Mark Lohman page 160: Nancy Hill page 161: davidduncanlivingston.com page 162: Eric Roth page 163: Tria Giovan page 164: davidduncanlivingston.com page 165: Nancy Hill page 166: Eric Roth page 167: davidduncanlivingston.com pages 168–170: Mark Lohman page 171: Tria Giovan pages 172–175: davidduncanlivingston.com page 176: Mark Lohman pages 177–180: davidduncanlivingston.com pages 181–183 : Mark Lohman page 184: *left* Mark Lohman; *right* Tria Giovan page 185: Mark Lohman pages 186–187: Phillip H. Ennis Photography page 188: *top* Phillip H. Ennis Photography; *bottom* davidduncanlivingston.com page 189: davidduncanlivingston.com pages–196: Mark Lohman page 197: *top* Mark Lohman; *bottom left* davidduncanlivingston.com pages 198–201: Mark Lohman page 218: Eric Roth

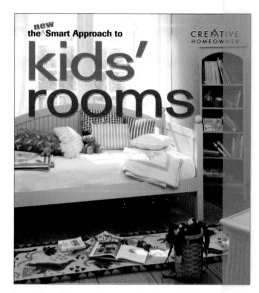